Tomislav Perko
1000 Days of Spring

Author
Tomislav Perko

Title
1000 Days of Spring

Subtitle
Travelogue of a hitchhiker

Translation
Anamarija Brzica

Editor
Daniel Edward Allen

Assistant editors
Julia Schmidt, Alexandra Zetes

Graphic design
Ivan Osman

Cover design
Miroslav Vujović

Photography
Tomislav Perko©

Photography editor
Caroline Perrier

Publisher
Self published

Printing studio
Printera Grupa

Time and place of publishing
Zagreb, 2014.

A CIP catalogue record for this book is
available in the Online Catalogue of the National
and University Library in Zagreb as 881869

ISBN 978-953-58060-1-1

The mark of
responsible forestry

1000 DAYS OF SPRING

(TRAVELOGUE OF A HITCHHIKER)

Self-published,
Zagreb, 2014.

For you.

PROLOGUE

Tomislav Perko refreshes the Croatian travel-writing scene, which, in the past ten years, has developed to the point where we could actually call it a movement. Perko has imposed himself as a leader of a new wave of travellers, but the huge success he has enjoyed did not come overnight. He entered the scene quite humbly, practically out of nowhere, as a young advocate of CouchSurfing. Thanks to his amazing adventurous spirit, which took him to the places on the globe most people couldn't imagine in their wildest dreams, and also to his human qualities, he has gathered an army of respected followers. Over the past few years, many generations of travel writers have fought their way through narrow media and literary passages, each of them offering their own, personal and original, story. Some of them climbed high on hardly accessible mountains, some of them walked for thousand kilometres, some of them travelled searching for beaches, others searching for fun, some of them cycled and some of them simply presented their great erudite capacities in the form of travel journals. However, while doing it, each and every one of them had a certain budget in order to realize their travelling projects. Perko offered the world his own version of travelling, with his thumb stuck out, a funfair in his head, a bomb in his lungs and, most importantly, with only a few coins in his pocket. He spent years wandering across the planet, met the most incredible people, experienced so many things that they would suffice for ten lifetimes, let alone the one he has.

You are holding in your hands Perko's literary debut, in which he completely opens up. He managed to transfer in writing, with his skilful writing techniques, and in a uniquely honest manner, his journey from a boy growing up in a traditional Croatian family, to a great traveller who feels at home wherever he goes. This travelogue is not only a warm and honest personal confession of man yearning for the Road, but is also an excellent guide for every young traveller who wants to discover the world. Having read this book, you will come to the conclusion that it only has one flaw – you will not be able to escape the wish to read the sequel to this warm and interesting story.

Hrvoje Šalković - Shale

Day 794.

"Our next guest is going to tell us how it is possible to travel with almost no money," Daniela announced. "Ladies and gentlemen, Tomislav Perko."

The audience got their cue for the applause, and the doors with the "8th floor" sign on them open in front of me. I enter the studio, climb the stage, shake hands with Daniela and sit in the red sofa in front of her.
I am nervous. After all, I am on one of the most popular Croatian TV shows, invited to talk about travelling with some other Croatian travel writers - people who began travelling long before I was allowed to put my foot out of the park without my mother's permission.
I've come to tell my story - the story about the last two years of my life, in ten minutes I was supposed to be on air.

"Tomislav, you are my youngest guest," Daniela began. "How old are you?"
"Twenty-five," I replied, exhaling deeply.
"You are in your final year of university," she continued.
"That's right. I have one more exam to pass before I graduate."
"You also have some working experience. Even though today you look quite casual in your hoodie, only recently you could easily be seen wearing a suit and a tie."
Recently. The notion of time is such a relative concept. I would bet my head that a lifetime has passed since that period of my life. Or a couple of them, as a matter of fact.
"Yes, I worked as a stockbroker and my lifestyle was completely different; I would dress nicely, save money and buy myself pretty things. Luckily, the financial crisis came..."

Day 1.

I'm sitting on a worn old couch still wearing my expensive suit, rolling a joint. That was my favourite action of a day: a few minutes of peace, tranquillity and silence. I considered it a reward after a hard day at work, especially after a day like this in which I've become aware of the hopeless situation in which I've found myself.

Only a couple of weeks ago everything seemed to be perfect. I was considered one of the most talented young stockbrokers on the market, with great intuition as far as the stock dealing market was concerned. The speed with which I dealt with the transactions earned me my nickname – *the fastest finger.*

I started with few thousand dollars, and only two years later I had a portfolio of almost a hundred grand. As I kept on increasing the initial amount of money, I had managed to convince my family and friends to invest, and when they invested money I would only take out more loans on their investments. I used to make promises to them saying that you couldn't lose on the stock market and that it would be a pity not to make use of such an opportunity to make easy money.

And they bought it.

It was all just a big game for me, another way to have fun, an adrenaline rush. The truth was that I didn't know anything about the stock market, financial reports or indicators. I was an economics student without any qualification to be a stockbroker, but I was excellent at hiding my own lack of knowledge. I would listen carefully to my older colleagues talk about the current events on the stock market: which are the most overrated stocks, which are the most underestimated ones; I would listen to them talk about the conditions on the foreign stock market and the expected movements. In that way, I would kill three birds with one stone: I earned their respect since they liked the feeling of being listened to and appreciated by someone; I avoided all the questions directed to me; and I would also use all their predictions about the stock market when a client asked me for a piece of advice.

I was a day trader; I was interested exclusively in short-term speculations, preferably completing transactions within a day. Many times I would walk out of work with a few hundred, or even a few thousand dollars more in my bank account. My personal record was three thousand bucks, which I earned in less than two hours. My moves, and they were often crazy moves, earned me respect among my colleagues.

In fact, I was a mere gambler who in high school started going around betting houses and later even visited roulette tables in casinos. I was addicted to the excitement and the unpredictability of those situations.

And then, as a freshman in college, I found a perfect replacement, not only approved by society, but even encouraged.

"I'm a stockbroker, you know," I used to say to the guys at university in order to excuse myself for being absent for most of my lectures and to justify my lifestyle. I wasn't a regular student like the others, I wasn't so keen on passing the exams, and I wasn't looking forward to getting a degree that would guarantee me a well-paid job and a good reputation. I already had all of those things.

The market kept on growing. Everyone was making serious money, new brokerage firms were opening almost on a daily basis, and there were so many investment funds and opportunities to make money.

And then the black September of 2008 came and everything changed.

The dramatic fall in real estate value, the collapse of the biggest banks in the world, the financial crisis... There was a sudden slump in the stock market, both in Croatia and worldwide. Some stocks dropped by 70 per cent. Many people even talked about it as the worst financial crisis in the past eighty years, about billions of lost dollars on a daily basis, and I heard for the first time the one word that no broker wants to hear – the word that rhymes with *dash*.

During those days we would only stare helplessly at the screens, holding our heads and counting our losses at the end of the day: ours, and those of our clients. People were losing their life savings in less than a couple of weeks. They would call us looking for some explanation, a way to fix things. But we had nothing to say to them.

The worst thing was that the same scenario kept on repeating from one day to another. The stock value kept on dropping and people could only watch as their money was lost in front of their very eyes. All of us were crazy, to say the least.

The only alternative was to sell everything you had, and in that way, end your suffering – save what was left to save.

That was exactly what I did. I sold all the stock I owned, closed all my margins and counted my losses.

35,000 dollars.

Thirty-five. Thousand. Dollars.

I lay back and light my joint.

Day 794.

I remember the feeling in my stomach that followed those days. In only a couple of weeks I managed to lose the same amount of money that one would earn in a few years' extremely hard work. Gone, just like that. And I was supposed to get it back somehow. The best way I could.

It all seemed unreal to me. Hopeless. Depressing.

"How can you say that it was a good thing that the financial crisis came?" Daniela wondered.

I recognized the perplexed look in her eyes. If someone had told me that losing all that money would be one of the things I'd be grateful for and that in two years' time I would consider that situation a positive one, I would have asked for some of the drug they were on. Cleary, it was good stuff.

However, in hindsight, I'm glad it happened.

"Well, I can, since that crisis completely changed my approach to life. When I lost all that money and the things I had grown accustomed to, I quit my job and got a job in a juice bar – that was the one thing that changed me completely."

Day 31.

"Martina, we need a student to work at the counter," I heard Mongoose, who was sitting at a table next to me, say, "we can no longer do it on our own."

The two of them were awesome. They were the owners of a juice bar in Zagreb where I used to go every day during my lunch break. It was only two minutes away from my office but it was enough to take a break from looking at all those screens, numbers and overall depression that, during those days, weeks and months, was a common thing in the office. The bar was my getaway.

"Maybe I could work here," I said putting down my strawberry smoothie on the painted wooden table.

They gave me a confused look, stopped for a moment and burst into laughter. I joined them not knowing where I'd got the idea from.

"Wait a minute," Martina started speaking, even though she was still laughing, "you're a stockbroker, right?"

"Yes, I am," I said cheerfully.

"You come here every day wearing a suit and a tie and you order a four-dollar juice?" she continued.

"That's right."

"And now you'd like to work at the counter and make the very same juices?"

"Yes."

"Are you a student?"

"Yes."

"How can you be student and a stockbroker, both at the same time?"

"It's a long story."

"How much do they pay you?"

"Seven bucks an hour, plus some other benefits."

"Like the suit you're wearing?"

"Like the suit I'm wearing, yes."

"And now you've come here to fuck with us," Mongoose interrupted her, "you know we can't give you half the money they pay you."

"Look," I started with the same serious tone he was using, "I like this place. I come here every day to take a break from all the shit at the office. I haven't seen anyone stressed out here. People come here with a smile on their face; they order a juice, pay for it, thank you for the service and drink it with pleasure. Yes, I would like to work here. I know you can't pay me the half the money they pay me, but I really don't care about that at the moment."

Mongoose got up from his table and sat next to me.

"Are you being serious?" He asked me.

"Dead serious," I replied.

"How much money would you be satisfied with?"

"I don't care about the money. I want to work and you can pay me how much you can."

"Okay, so it wouldn't be a problem for you if you worked for free?" He was provoking me, looking me directly in the eyes.

"Nope." I accepted the game with a smile on my face, not breaking eye contact.

It lasted for around ten seconds.

"Be here tomorrow at ten to eight," he said returning to Martina, "your hourly wage will be three dollars fifty."

I finished my smoothie and got back to the office. Calls from angry clients, red numbers on the screens, bad news on every Internet site. Just a regular day at the office.

I took a pen and a piece of paper, drew a line in the middle and wrote BROKERAGE FIRM on one side and JUICE BAR on the other side. The tension at work on one side, and the relaxed atmosphere on the other. Unsatisfied and nervous clients with a lot of demands, as opposed to careless and happy clients. Work in front of a computer and work behind the counter on the other side. Suit and tie on one hand, and casual clothes that make me feel free on the other hand. Hourly wage of seven dollars plus benefits on one side, and minimal wage that would suffice to pay the rent and hopefully bills.

Life does have an interesting sense of humour. For the past couple of years my life came down to managing money, but the roles, in fact, were reversed – money was managing me. I realized how limited my life had been and how governed by money, especially now that I didn't have any.

I fell into a trap. I've been saving money, and each day I was looking for a new way to make some more, to buy something new, to treat myself to something nice. No matter how convinced I was that I was in charge in that relationship, I was wrong. As always, I had to learn by my own mistakes. The hard way. Thirty-five thousand times harder.

Money. The only reason for keeping my current job.

I threw another quick glance at what I'd written down, took off my tie, got up, knocked on my boss's office door and quit my job.

"I'm out, guys," I informed my colleagues as soon as I left the boss's office. They weren't surprised since they had also begun looking for other jobs, a way out of the chaos. They were only waiting for the first person to totally lose it and run away from it all. Of course, I was the one – the youngest and in the biggest trouble.

I decided to walk back home. I bought myself a beer and lay down in the middle of the park looking at the sky.

"From now on, the stock market is history for me." I made myself a promise, knowing that gamblers usually try to dig their way out of the crap they get themselves into with - more gambling.

I took a sip of beer and I felt better. I felt as if I had just broken up with a girlfriend in whom I'd had no interest in for a while, but I kept on finding the same stupid reasons not to break up with her. Yes, I was leaving that relationship so deeply scarred that the scars wouldn't fade away for a long time, if they ever did manage to fade away. Still, I was leaving it.

And tomorrow, at ten to eight, I had a date with a new, more exciting, happier and healthier, although poorer, girl. I was hoping that she would help me get over my ex.

I got up, looked at the green patch on the back part of my pants and carelessly headed to my home.

Day 87.

"Why do they call you Mongoose?" I asked my boss one evening while we were in a secret room in The Jazz Club. We would hang out there until morning, playing poker. The atmosphere reminded me of old mafia movies. We were invisible to the other guests of the bar, hidden in a smoky room where we would drink, smoke and play cards.

Even though I was only a worker in the juice bar, very soon I started feeling as if I were a part of the family. After only a few days I started calling Martina sis, and she called me bro. I was happy with my new job and with my new employers, and I could tell that they were also satisfied with me.

I enjoyed going to work, always did my job with a smile on my face: I enjoyed preparing freshly squeezed juices, having small talk with the clients, and at the end of the day I cleaned the machines, scrubbed the floors and cleaned the toilets. I got an opportunity to meet people whose lives were different, more interesting and more special. They would talk about art, travelling and healthy living. You would never meet a guy who placed himself at the counter with a beer in his hand, gossiping about the locals. You would never sense the nervousness and the constant talk about money, which I grew accustomed to in my last job. I made a couple of new friends and went with them to the theatre, barbecued with them in the suburbs of Zagreb, and Martina, Mongoose and I became so close that every night, after closing they would take me to grab a beer.

We would place ourselves at the counter and talk about the local gossip.

"I grew up in Maksimir,"[1] Mongoose started, "and back in those days everyone had a nickname that came from a zoo animal. So, one day as I was checking out what was going on, I stretched my neck and turned my head around and one of the older boys noticed it saying that I reminded him of a mongoose – and that's about it."

I listened attentively to his stories about how it felt growing up on the streets of Zagreb, messing around with your buddies, being at the legendary football matches of Dinamo Zagreb, experiencing and surviving such things as your closest friend's overdose, and how he was saved that

---

[1] A neighborhood in Zagreb that is home to the zoo, and also the football stadium of Dinamo Zagreb.

day when he met Martina with whom he went to Ireland.

They remained there for five years.

I found it interesting to hear his story: it was funny how someone who had grown up in the same city as I had, had a completely different childhood. Compared to his, my childhood was so innocent and careless that I often thought if I were ever to write a book about my life it would open with the following sentence: I grew up in a fairy tale.

I remember the days in which my family would move from one apartment to the other and the days spent playing in a park in front of the building. My brother and I weren't allowed to leave the park so that our mother could always keep an eye on us. I remembered how I'd spent time in the school playground playing football or basketball with my best friends when I was going to the elementary school. I remembered all those video games that were popular back when I was finishing elementary school, which were the reason for my spending so many hours in front of a computer screen, lost in another world. I remembered how I was never one of those guys who smoked, drank, fought or chased girls. My first kiss was on my last day in the elementary school and I only did it so that I wouldn't leave the elementary school without having the memory of a first kiss. Perhaps I should have. I remembered Katarina, with whom I spent three years in high school, three years of spending every recess together, three years of walking her to the bus stop. I remembered enrolling at the university and nearly dropping out after the first lectures.

I was still a kid, barely out of my first serious relationship, without any vices, without any friends, I didn't know what I wanted to do with myself or who I wanted to be one day. Consequently, depending on the people I hung around with, I passed through different phases.

First, I was into fast cars despite the fact that, at that time, I was driving my brother's old VW Golf. I started going out: sometimes I would simply hang around in a park with a bottle of beer in my hand, and sometimes I would go out to fancy places. I gave playing the guitar a try because I wanted to win over a girl who had a beautiful voice and she played guitar very well. I gave it up about at the same time I gave her up. One Saturday I went to Maksimir stadium to the north stands, among the Bad Blue Boys[2] because the brother of my girlfriend at that time was a passionate supporter of Dinamo Zagreb.

Even though Dinamo was playing some unimportant match, when I

---

[2] Dinamo Zagreb fans, known for trouble

heard the roar of the grandstand and the synchronized rhythm of the drums, palms and a couple of thousand voices - that was it. Just like that, I had a new hobby, a new place to which I belonged. I didn't miss a single match at Maksimir stadium, and I would usually go on my own to the matches. The game itself and the score usually didn't matter, all that mattered was never to save your voice, support the team on the field, be the twelfth player and feel the great energy in the stands.

Soon I started going to away matches. Twenty-eight hours of suffering in a bus to France, during which I witnessed the biggest drug consumption ever, even before we reached the Slovenian border. I witnessed gas stations being robbed and the ravage through the city looking for the supporters of the local club. Finally, I found myself on the stand reserved for the supporters of the guest team, among the guys from the bus, who were using chairs and flares to fight the cops. I, coughing from all the tear gas around me, was texting my mother telling her that I was okay, safe and sound.

I also went to Norway, by myself, where, after a couple of days spent travelling and a considerable amount of beer, I slept through the whole match, in the bus in front of the stadium. I think I am the only supporter ever who managed to do something like that. I also witnessed one of the greatest victories of my club: the one against Ajax, in the middle of Amsterdam, which marked the end of my travels following Dinamo.

Dinamo will be playing against Ajax: the match that will decide who makes it to the UEFA Cup – the headline was on every Internet site. I left everything I was doing at that moment and sent a group message to the guys I thought would definitely be attracted by going to Amsterdam, as I was. It was a beautiful city, with rich history and culture and my friends definitely wanted to see that.

"Sure thing," they answered unanimously.

We watched the first match together, in the north stand at Maksimir. We cheered the team on hoping for a positive result so that we would be left with at least a glimpse of hope for the return match. The match was marked by the beautiful pass by our player Schildenfeld to an Ajax player, who set the final score, 0:1.

Already accustomed to the terrible results of my team when it came to the European competitions, I wasn't that devastated by the defeat. I was still looking forward to the return match even though I knew that I would only be watching my team losing another season in the UEFA cup. "Whether they win or lose, we're always here" was one of the Bad Blue Boys mottoes. Still, it appeared that, after all, I would be alone. My friends, one by one, kept on finding excuses not to go. There was less than a week until match day.

Pussies.

"Why don't you go on your own?" Nina asked me. She was the one I usually went to in the situations like that to whine a bit.

Nina is my colleague from the university. In fact, she is much more than a colleague. She is the person who accepted a spoilt, stubborn and narrow-minded human being and, by asking questions, leading by her own example and by giving unconditioned love, made him observe the world in a different light, in a more open way. She is the person who started making a person out of me.

"On my own?" I gave her a look of panic. "What would I do there on my own?"

"Trust me, you'll have better time than you do when you go with the others." She answered self-assuredly. "Anyway, if you always wait for the others to do something, you'll never do anything."

I was sure she knew what she was talking about. During the first of the lectures at university where we sat together, she showed me some of the photos from her journey to India, Brazil and Portugal. She was a couple of years older than me and very different, but despite our differences, or maybe because of them, we got along very well. I could see the excitement, unpredictability, and adventure – all those things that were waiting for me if I decided to go on my own – in her eyes. It was wonderful. And a bit terrifying. I was afraid of being alone somewhere out there, far away, left on my own.

"How about you go with me?" I was giving her a puppy look.

"Haha, no way," she said briskly, "it's your journey, don't go looking for an easy way out. When you do something on your own, without anyone's help, the feeling is much better."

"I can't wait to see the look in your eyes when you come back." I could still hear her last sentence while I was waiting in line at the main train station to buy the ticket to Amsterdam, while I was buying a large backpack and a sleeping bag; and also while I was waiting in line in front of the stadium to buy the ticket for the match. I was ready to go.

I didn't have to wait for a long time for the adventure to begin. As I entered the train I spotted two guys who were, just like me, going to the match. They treated me to some wine, while I offered them with some bread from the student restaurant. As soon as we got sober again, the German conductor, with the help of the local police, threw me off the train, somewhere near Duisburg, saying that my ticket was *"falsch."* However, after a few hours I finally arrived in A'dam. I moved into Jeff and Andy's place, two guys I'd come across CouchSurfing, a social network I'd known for only a few months. During the following few days I lived in the very centre of the city, in an apartment that was situated above a store owned by Jeff and Andy that sold more than 300 types of beer, wine and liquor.

As a true local, I had my own bike. I went sightseeing around the beautiful canals and observed the houses that looked very lively even if you weren't high. I met a couple of new friends, borrowed a guitar from a street musician and played in front of an unknown crowd for the first time in my life. I witnessed a match in which my team won 3:2, which was one of the biggest victories in the history of the club.

Still, the moment I will remember for the rest of my life happened just after the match. I was at the apartment, thirsty, hungry and exhausted. I had 120 minutes of clapping and yelling behind me, especially since we weren't allowed to bring drums inside the stadium. And I had fried crispy chicken, salty French fries with ketchup and a bottle of Fanta in front of me. I dug in as if it was my last meal. At the peak of my hedonistic experience I took the lid of the plastic cup off and realized that the liquid inside of it was black. They gave me Coke instead of Fanta.

My entire world crashed.

"Ok, the situation is like this" – I started a monologue after a minute of shock – "you're dying of thirst and you despise Coke. The nearest supermarket is a galaxy away. There is nothing interesting in the fridge. Is there any chance that just a for a moment you try to imagine that the black liquid in front of you is, in fact, the most appealing drink in the world and try to enjoy it? Huh?"

I shushed the spoilt brat within me, closed my eyes, concentrated on the action, pulled the cup and took a sip.

It worked.

While I was chewing the chicken wing and drinking the soda I asked myself one thing: if I can make myself love something that I normally don't like with the power of my will, what else can I change in the same way? Do I have to put everything I've learnt, everything I've experienced so far into question? That included the opinions I'd been building all those years – should I start all over again? Could I see life with different eyes, taste it with a different mouth, with a different being?

That moment was the peak of my journey, and after that trip I didn't want to travel with Dinamo anymore, but instead I wanted to look for other enlightening experiences, no matter that I might have to endure many banal experiences to find them.

"Tom, my friend," Mongoose interrupted me, "you can learn all sorts of things when you travel. Fuck school, fuck university: life is the best teacher you can ever have. Life is outside our borders: geographical, moral and traditional. When you travel, you're forced to forget everything you've ever learnt, you're forced to recognize the illusion created within you by society, family, school, church and tradition. When you travel, you're completely free: there is no one to judge your actions, only you are the judge of your actions. That is the one thing you will find when travelling: the true you. You will find your answers once you accumulate enough life experience. You can read books, watch documentaries, have serious conversations with your friends in the smoky back room of The Jazz Club, but it won't mean a thing, not until you head off and start learning by creating your own examples and making your own mistakes. Remember that."

Day 794.

No matter how many times I told my Amsterdam story about Coke and Fanta, nobody seemed to understand it. They found it incredible that the most important thing from my first trip on my own, after a couple of days spent in a city like Amsterdam, after witnessing one of the biggest matches ever, was the simplest realization that I could easily change something I'd learnt.

Because of this, I kept the most important story to myself. I was the only one who could perceive it in the right light.

"About at the same time I started working at the juice bar I started hosting people via CouchSurfing..."

"What is CouchSurfing?" Daniela kept on interrupting me.

"CouchSurfing is an online community of people who host other people in their homes."

It would be impossible to describe in a single sentence my countless experiences with CS. How can one retell the years that I spent with people in my or their homes exchanging stories, jokes and deep conversation? How can one retell the nights spent hanging out together, sleepless nights, nights during which I connected with the people on the next couch?

"So, basically, you offer someone a couch to spend the night on it?"

"A couch, bed, place on the floor, depending on the space you have."

An image of a guy sleeping on my kitchen floor surrounded by twenty bottles of beer and a few empty pizza boxes flashed in front of my eyes. The good old days.

"So, they get a place to stay and a meal?"

"A place to stay, yes, and sometimes a meal, a drink or something else. That depends on the situation. The thing about CouchSurfing is not that it's free, it's about making new friends and meeting the culture you're about to explore from the perspective of a local. In that sense, I've been host to more than one hundred people. During the last year, year and a half I've started travelling myself. One day I went to Sofia..."

Day 186.

"Good day." The postman entered the juice bar one sunny afternoon. "Does Hrvoje Šalković[3] live here?"

We were cleaning up the mess left by the customers during the lunch break. Martina, Mongoose and I exchanged confused looks: we didn't get it. Only a few days ago I'd given them a copy of the book that this guy wrote. Nina had given it to me, couple of weeks earlier, and it made me wonder, already after the first chapter:

In the deep space there is a tiny bluish planet called Earth. People, mammals that like to call themselves rational beings, live there. The planet Earth revolves stringently and strenuously around its axis. People revolve stringently and strenuously around their habits. They are born, they grow up, they grow old and they die never giving up on that routine. During that journey some important stuff happens to them: they love, make mistakes, chatter, get involved, lie, fornicate, write, repent, have guilty consciences, forget, are afraid. However, most of the people are just born; they grow up, grow old and die. Most of them take these events for granted, as something that should necessarily happen in that sequence and they do not even think about it. Most people live their lives just to get it over with without taking a moment to think about life.

In the deep space there is a planet Earth and people live on it. Some of them have dreams. These people spend their lives searching endlessly for their personal piece of tranquillity. There is only a handful of these people and not rarely are they despised and lonely. They call them dreamers. They say to them that it's high time they grew up and stopped acting as if they were still children. So, most of the dreamers end up with their dreams crushed and they give up their search for tranquillity. Only the most strenuous among them never give up because deep down they know that no government, no law, no authority should stand between them and their dreams.

I read the whole book in one fell swoop. So I started thinking about it. What would be my way to tranquillity?

---

[3] famous Croatian writer, also known as Shale.

I was still thinking about it when the postman entered the bar and asked about the author of the book that made me think about the whole thing in the first place. A coincidence? I don't believe in coincidences.

The postman informed me that this writer lived nearby so I decided to use that information as soon as my shift was over. I buzzed on his intercom.

"Who's there?" I heard the voice.

"Let's go grab a beer."

"Who is it?"

"You don't know me, but I know you. I've read your book, I've come across your address by accident so I've decided to invite you to have a beer with me."

"So, just like that, you've decided to invite an unknown man to have a beer with you?"

"I read your book, you've done some crazier things than this."

"Hmm, that's true."

"I need your help in finding tranquillity."

"What?"

"Oh, nothing. We can talk about it over a beer."

"Look, I appreciate the invitation, but at the moment I'm not in the mood to have a beer with a stranger. Also, I have some problems at home, so...maybe some other time."

"Yeah, maybe."

I didn't find the author of my favourite book that nice anymore. As I saw it, he should've run down the stairs, burst into laughter, give me a hug, congratulated me on my courage and gone to get wasted with me.

"If I ever happen to become a successful writer I will never reject an invitation for a beer," I said to Martina and Mongoose the following day, after I told them about my failed intercom conversation. I sounded like a hurt teenage girl.

"What could he possibly say to you that you don't already know?" Mongoose asked me while preparing a freshly squeezed orange juice. "You've read his book and you liked it. If you really think that you've found yourself in that book, do the same thing as its protagonist did. Just go. How many times have you told me that fucking story about the Coke and Fanta in Amsterdam? And you still don't seem to get the point. All that talk doesn't mean anything if you don't DO something. Don't go looking for excuses, advice or courage. You'll find it on your way, just like you've read in the book."

"How can I travel if I don't have any money?" – I started with the excuses – "it was easy to go to Amsterdam when I still had all that money from the stocks. Now, I can barely pay the rent and bills. Don't get me started on debt..."

"To hell with the money," he left the oranges and approached me, "take a few days off the next week. Here, take some money and go somewhere."

When I came home that day, four Bulgarians were waiting for me in front of the door.

For a few months my roommate and I had been hosting travellers via CS in our subtenant apartment. Our apartment was a place where people could take a rest, wash themselves, eat and drink. It was a place that offered them an opportunity to get to know the culture from a different perspective and it was all for free. So many people had passed through our apartment that our neighbours, as soon as they spotted someone with a big backpack in our neighbourhood, they would instantly take them to our door. We had a huge world map on the wall and we could easily spend days looking at it as if it was a television. And we would fantasize.

Even though that the experience was very beneficial for our guests it was also good for us. Nearly every evening in our living room we were surrounded by people who were living their dreams, who travelled the world and in whose eyes you could see that they were doing what they wanted to do. Those were the guys who would tell us their first-hand experiences over a beer or two. It couldn't be compared to any book, any documentary or a film: we had people in the flesh in front of us who were telling us about their travelling experiences: one guy travelled for more than ten years, another travelled by bike from France to China, and one hitchhiked from Germany to Iran, all of them finding occasional jobs on their way that kept them going. Those were the people who weren't limited by the routine and habits imposed by the society in which we live. Those were the people without any prejudice or hatred, but were only full of understanding.

They lived their lives in the best way they could. Simple. Could they be my inspiration and give me a piece of advice?

"Sofia isn't far away," Vasil told me when I announced that I would be having a few days off soon and that I wanted to use them for a short journey. "We would be pleased to host you."

"The only problem is the money," I complained. "I only have 40 Euros, which my boss gave me. What can I do with 40 Euros?"

"Trust me, a lot of things," he carried on carelessly. "Beer costs less than a Euro there. The food is even less expensive, and you won't have to pay for the accommodation."

"How will I get there?" I kept on asking more questions, or maybe looking for new excuses.

"Have you ever hitchhiked?" Elena, his girlfriend, asked me. Everyone else was waiting for my response.

"I haven't," I said sadly.

"So, obviously, now's the time." They laughed and raised their glasses. Obviously.

Day 189.

I was awake even before the alarm went off at 6:04.

I put my backpack on and took two pieces of card that said SLAVONSKI BROD, BELGRADE, NIŠ and SOFIA[4]. I took bus number 276 to Ivanja Reka and got off at the last stop. I had to cross the fields and a stream, and climb over a fence in order to get to the toll booths going east.

The nervousness was definitely there. The fear. I was sure that I was breaking at least one law by walking along the highway. God knew what was ahead of me: what kind of drivers, what would be my experience in Serbia and in Bulgaria. I had eight hundred kilometres ahead of me, and no plan B. My head was a complete mess and my heart kept on beating heavily. I could still easily give it all up and go back home, lie back on my comfortable sofa, in the familiar surroundings, go back to my friends and to my nights out.

"Hey, you!" I heard someone calling me just as I was dropping my backpack on the road, between the toll booths.

I haven't even started hitchhiking and I'm already being chased away. It was a bad sign.

I turned around and saw a guy in a dark blue VW waving at me through an open window.

"I'm going to Slavonski Brod," he shouted, "you can come with me."

I immediately ran to the car, threw the backpack on the back seat and sat in the front.

"I saw from the sign on your backpack that you were headed for Slavonski Brod," he was saying as he took his ticket at the toll booth, "my car horn doesn't function so I had to shout."

"And I thought that I was being chased away from here," I replied as I secured the seat belt. "This is my first time hitchhiking and you pulled over before I even got the chance to stick out my thumb."

"It sounds like a good sign." He stepped on the gas and changed gear. "Besim, nice to meet you."

"Tomislav." We shook hands. "Nice to meet you, too."

I observed the highway in front of me while the thoughts were piling up inside my head. Is it possible that this has just happened? I haven't even stuck out my thumb and I already have a ride for the next two hun-

---

[4] Four big cities on the way.

dred kilometres. Have I just made a world record in hitchhiking? Has this been a sheer luck or coincidence or a sign of something?

"Wanna beer?" Besim distracted me, "there's one in the glove compartment."

It was only then that I realized that the guy was holding a beer bottle between his legs and that he was sipping it slowly. He was driving and sipping a beer. At 7am. Maybe this hadn't been the smartest move I could've made.

I opened the drawer and saw another small bottle. I took it, thanked him, opened it and took a sip. If I drank it, he wouldn't. At least that was something.

Besim was a construction worker from Bosnia working temporarily in Slovenia. We talked about life, work and war. I liked him. I observed him driving with a beer in his hand, slowly, in the right lane of the highway without overtaking anyone. I was relieved. I was in safe hands.

"Hey, let's make a stop at this gas station," I suggested. "Let me buy you a beer; after all, we have to celebrate my first hitchhiking experience."

He laughed, took a right turn, and soon we were sharing four large cans of beer.

"Do you smoke?" He asked, taking a pack of cigarettes placed next to the gear stick.

"Thank you, but I don't smoke cigarettes." I accentuated the word *cigarettes*.

Besim was one of those people who know why. Soon we made another stop to roll a joint, after which we moved on. It was 8am.

I had a goofy grin on my face and my head started moving up and down following the rhythm of a rock song that was playing on the radio. I couldn't believe what was happening, who I was with, where I was. If someone had told me a story in which a person hitchhikes for the first time, stops a car before he even sticks out his thumb, shares six beers with the driver and smokes a joint with him I wouldn't have believed it. And the exact same thing had happened to me in the past hour or two. Things couldn't get any more extreme, intense or weird.

"My friend," Besim interrupted my thoughts, "have you ever tried speed?"

I got out at the west exit from Slavonski Brod. There wasn't a living soul at the toll booths, but I couldn't care less. The sun was shining brightly, my head was spinning, I danced cheerfully by the road, thanking the sky for my first amazing hitchhiking experience.

A few cars drove past me, but they were all going back to Zagreb. Still the smile wasn't leaving my face. After an hour I got a bit more serious, and after two hours I started frowning. After three hours I was getting desperate.

I was way too naive. What was I thinking: going like that without a plan or a backup plan, hitchhiking to a city that was eight hundred kilometres away with only forty Euros in my pockets. A true optimist. I was thinking about returning to Zagreb and of giving it all up. I still had a story that I could retell for the rest of my life.

When my pessimism reached its peak, as usually happens, one guy pulled over and gave me a ride across the Serbian border, showed me around Belgrade and left me in the best place to continue hitchhiking – toll booths on the highway that led to Niš. I continued my journey with a Macedonian truck driver who left me at a big gas station in the middle of the highway. I was half way there, and in theory, I still had plenty of time to get to Sofia in time. In theory.

The clouds were starting to gather, it was starting to rain. It was getting darker. I gave up asking the truck drivers for a lift since I realized that they could only get me to the border. Also, I gave up asking cars, which could only give me a ride to Niš where I would be left in the middle of the road, at the mercy of rain and darkness. I could either bump into someone going straight to Sofia or spend the night here and continue the following day.

When you're at a gas station and your possibilities are limited to those people who are headed for a town that is three hundred kilometres away and in another country, there's a high chance you're going to spend quite a lot of time there. Also, you will be thinking about a vast spectrum of feelings you'd felt that day. The fear of first hitchhiking, the luck in breaking the world record in finding a ride, the shock of the amount of mood altering substances consumed early in the morning, the desperation due to spending three hours in one place, the satisfaction of finding a ride to Belgrade, and, finally, depression because it seemed that I would be spending the night at a gas station in the middle of Serbia.

However, luck hadn't abandoned me yet: it came to me in the shape of a car with Bulgarian licence plates. Finally, some hope. I made the saddest face I could, walked around the car with my sign saying the name of the Bulgarian capital while the driver and his co-driver were paying the bill. They were approaching the car. They spotted me. They said something to each other, sat in the car, started it and got going. They pulled over next to me and rolled down the window.

"Where are you from?"

"Croatia."

"You're headed for Sofia?"

"Yes."

"Get in."

I was the luckiest man on Earth.

The ride across the south of Serbia, a downpour the likes of which I had never seen before, the most delicious *burek*[5] in a bakery in Niš, lightning that illuminated the terrifying canyons we were passing through, stray dogs as we were crossing the border in the middle of the night, arriving in Sofia way after midnight, finding Vasil at a party – I did it!

What followed after that were gloomy nights with my Bulgarian friends, climbing up mount Vitosha in the rain, night camping and *sarma*[6] and sleeping in a cramped tent, morning climbing up a 50-metres rock despite my fear of heights, giving free hugs in the centre of the city during the day, hanging all night in dark parks under the influence of unknown hallucinogens, meeting new people and strengthening the relationships with the people I already knew.

Four days and forty Euros later I was at the metro station begging for one *lev* to buy a ticket so I could get out of town and start hitchhiking again. I couldn't try to go into the metro without a ticket because the conductor was standing by the entrance.

"Do you speak English?" I asked the first girl that seemed that she might have mercy on me and give me one *lev*.

She nodded her head up and down, turned around and left. Four days in Bulgaria weren't enough to get used to their body language: nodding their head up and down meant *no*, and right and left meant *yes*.

"Good afternoon," I approached a guy who seemed approximately my age, "I'm from Croatia, I'm hitchhiking in order to get back home and I need one *lev* to buy a ticket to get out of town. Can you help me?"

"Croatia?" he replied, "where from?"

"Zagreb."

---

[5] A kind of a traditional cheese pie.

[6] A kind of traditional dish of cabbage leaves rolled around a filling usually based on minced meat, popular in the Balkans.

"Riiiight," he smiled widely, "Dinamo Zagreb?"

"Yes, Dinamo Zagreb." I started laughing, too, surprised by the fact that a random passer-by in Sofia recognized the name of a football club from Zagreb. He took two tickets out of his pocket and inserted them in the machine.

"Dinamo Zagreb!" we kept on yelling as we went inside the metro hugging each other, while other passengers looked at us surprised.

Sofia is really an ugly town, I started thinking as I was passing through the dirty suburbs searching for a good place to stick out my thumb. Grey and damaged buildings, broken muddy roads, and more than anything, during my whole time there, I was followed by drizzle. However, I had a blast in Sofia, thanks to all those people who took care of me, took me with them on all kinds of activities, who helped me to feel like a local, and not just a regular tourist who only passes through.

Apparently, it didn't matter where I was, but who I was with.

"Where are you going?" An older guy in his Yugo asked me when I was on the Bulgarian-Serbian border. A jolly truck driver from a village in the south of Serbia brought me there, but since he spent hours at the border I passed across on foot and started hitchhiking again.

"To Niš," I replied briefly.

"Get in," he responded in the same way.

I got into a car that was nearly falling apart, and the first thing I noticed was the face of the most notorious and wanted man from our area in the mirror – the war[7] criminal Ratko Mladić.

Only a hundred meters before I'd seen his face on a poster at the customs office offering a reward of a million dollars to those who were in possession of any kind of information about him. Maybe that guy knew something so we could split the reward?

I wasn't at ease. I didn't even introduce myself to him not knowing how he would react to a fact that he had Tomislav from Croatia in the car with him. However, in a matter of seconds, I came up with a whole story, just in case. I had a name that could easily pass on both sides of the border, I was a child from mixed marriage, my father was from Serbia, mother from Croatia. The father had died before the war started and my mother decided to go back to her family so we remained in Croatia.

It wasn't my fault that I was a Croat, I swear!

Luckily, the man wasn't up to talking too much so I even managed to

---

[7] Croatian War of Independence (1991-1995), fought between Croats and Serbs.

doze off a bit, waking up every now and then, just checking whether we were still on the highway or whether we took a turn to a village or somewhere else, God forbid.

"Thank you very much," I said to him when he left me by the toll booths near Niš. He gave me a strange look. I guess my accent[8] was a bit off. It didn't matter: I was safe, outside of his car.

I'd already prepared myself to wait at the toll booths: there wasn't much traffic, but it had started to rain so I had to go inside the office, where people working there treated me to a juice and listened to a shortened version of my four-day adventure.

I wasn't in a hurry since I knew that I had a place to crash in Belgrade, in case I got stuck there and didn't manage to get back to Zagreb in one day. On my way to Sofia I realized that it was always a good thing to have a plan B.

However, as it turned out, I didn't need one after all. The next driver who showed mercy on me was a Bulgarian who was going to Germany. I made myself comfortable, sent a message to my host in Belgrade saying that I wouldn't be visiting her and after only thirteen hours since I'd left Sofia I was back on my blue sofa in Zagreb.

It was incredible that the last time I was on the very same couch was only five days ago. So many things had happened since.

My eyes were wide open, the smile on my face was larger, and there was more air in the lungs. I collected stories, I was in situations that would usually never happen to me in my home town. In only five days I gathered enough material to tell stories for the next few years. Apparently, hitchhiking wasn't only a free way to get somewhere, it was also an excellent way to experience unusual things. Just like CouchSurfing. People hear about these ways of travelling first of all because they are free, but once they try them they discover there is more to it than simply being free.

Much more.

Plus, four days in a town eight hundred kilometres from Zagreb cost me exactly forty Euros, the same amount of money Mongoose had given to me. It was much less than the cost of living when I was in Zagreb. Is there a way to always live like that: intensely, excitingly, with a lot of changes, always meeting new people, new places, experiencing different things?

I wanted my life to be the exact same way it was during those four

---

[8] Croats and Serbs speak more or less the same language, just with different accents.

days. All the time. I wanted to leave and travel the world without ever stopping. Without having a home, a steady job, a return date. I wanted to be as free as a bird.

Still, there were two huge obstacles in front of me: unfinished university and the debt of thirty-five thousand dollars.

Despite my determination I couldn't find a (legal) way to earn that amount of money, so all I could do was focus on the first problem. The mitigating circumstance was that the people I was in debt to were family and friends, not loan sharks; family and friends who were, although let down on my part, supporting and full of understanding.

"You'll pay us back when you can," they used to say. "Finish university, get a job, take it easy. Don't worry too much. Everything will be okay."

That night was the first time I fell asleep peacefully, with confidence that everything would be all right.

Day 217.

My roommate and I kept on hosting people via the CS network. By re-telling me the stories from their journeys, my guests not only reinforced within me the wish to adopt travelling as a lifestyle, but they also gave me an idea of how to repay my debt. I was particularly intrigued by my guests from Australia, who told me that the minimum hourly wage in Australia was approximately AUD$15. The situation was similar in Scandinavia. The wages were a bit lower in Canada and in the USA, but an option was start-ing to appear: finishing school and finding a job abroad. I could spend a year or two abroad, live off of bread and water and earn enough money to repay my debt. After that I would finally be free to do what I want.

It was an excellent plan. Still, I had to finish university first and pass the remaining exams. I had to concentrate on studying and studying alone. I had to avoid anything that could prevent me from reaching my goal.

I had to stop hosting people. Even though juggling between studying for my exams and hanging around with the strangers in my apartment was fun, it wasn't very productive; especially since I didn't know how to say 'no' even when I had to.

On one hand, I knew I had to help them, after all, I would also need all the help I could get once on the road: that was the mantra I kept on repeating – I was buying good karma for the future. On the other hand, I had to take a rational decision and sort out my priorities, at least during the exam sessions.

I was quitting. I would only host an Australian girl who was com-ing that day and that would be final. I was taking a break of a couple of months, for a greater cause.

The doorbell rang. I opened the door. A blonde girl stood in front of me, smiling at me innocently, she looked me straight into the eyes and said:

"Hi, I'm Chloe."

Day 794.

"To Sofia?" Daniela asked me, "that's the name of some girl or?"

"No, Sofia is the capital of Bulgaria," I replied. Daniela was funny. Without knowing it she had touched upon a totally different story...

"After my trip to Sofia," I continued, "I started travelling around Croatia..."

Day 229.

Still not a word from her.

Without giving it much thought and without much planning I stuffed my backpack with some basic things, I went to the toll booths in the southern part of Zagreb and headed off towards the coast.

It was the middle of the summer, Zagreb was almost empty, and I had a few days off at work, thanks to a known Croatian tradition of taking long weekends, and thanks to the kindness of my bosses.

I visited my friends in Zadar, the same guys I now felt extremely grateful to for leaving me to go to Amsterdam alone. God only knows if things would've turned out the same way if I hadn't gone there on my own and if I hadn't walked into that fast food joint and gotten Coke instead of Fanta.

I went to Ričice, my mother's home village, where I used to spend a couple of weeks every summer when I was a child. That was the first time I went there on my own; that is, by using my thumb. It was interesting to arrive there and observe the beauty of the area from a different perspective, with different eyes. I started noticing all those little things that I'd been missing before, laid back in the car, having fun with family and friends, taking the beauty of the area for granted.

And its beauty was breathtaking. The Dalmatian debris, stone houses, greenery on both sides of the road, a cute little village with a small hill in the middle and an accumulation lake. Since the Red and Blue lakes[9] were only a few tens of kilometres away, it wasn't difficult to name that lake - Green lake. Above the lake, which was actually of a rich green colour, was a quarry in the shape of stairs: when we were children we thought it was a giant stairway.

It was a wonderful little place that I'd been looking at for all those years without actually seeing it. Even my grandma's *oblatne*[10] tasted better.

I visited Široki Brijeg, my father's home town in Herzegovina, another place I visited regularly every year, but which was now more colourful, more lively; my small cousins were more playful and the conversations with my family members were more intimate.

---

[9] Karst lakes near the city of Imotski.
[10] Traditional chocolate cake.

"What the fuck are you wearing?" my uncle asked me, referring to my style, which had changed significantly since the last time we saw each other. I was wearing light Nepalese fishing pants, made in Thailand and bought in an Indian shop in Zagreb; my haircut was asymmetrical: on one side I had something that appeared to be a tail, but it was only a moment of inspiration of a friend who did my hair for free, "you look like a faggot."

"What's wrong with faggots?" I asked, smiling provocatively. I knew that I shouldn't get into a fight with people who had grown up in a conservative Catholic environment but I simply couldn't let it go. I kept my tone peaceful with strong arguments hoping that the conversation wouldn't grow into a serious fight, knowing from the very start that the discussion was doomed. Strangely, I was having fun; I grew closer to the people I had those conversations with. I wasn't a coward who agreed with everything people would say, I wasn't afraid of speaking my mind and dealing with the consequences, I didn't care about what other people said after I was gone. I believe that was the reason why I earned their respect, even though they would never agree with me.

"Have you ever met a faggot?" I continued. "Well, I have and, actually, they're quite nice people."

"You are a faggot" – that was his response. I could sense that the conversation was turning into a fight so I gave up. I changed the subject and went to sleep soon after that.

I woke up early the next morning and decided to move on: I wanted to go towards the seaside.

I was leaving my father's hometown satisfied. I knew that everything was exactly the same as the last time I was there. Only one thing could've changed – me. I liked the new me, I liked how the new me observed the world, noticing the details, having an attitude.

"I'm not going to the coast, but you can come with me to Čavoglave," the driver who picked me up near Imotski told me, "after the celebration I'm going to the island of Pag so I can leave you there."

He was a war veteran who didn't have a left leg. He was quiet and withdrawn, but friendly. He was off to Čavoglave[11], to the celebration of Victory Day: the expected number of the visitors was 100,000. The celebration was supposed to be accompanied by a concert by Thompson, a guy known for his right-wing political attitude.

---

[11] A famous village in Croatia known for the bravery of its people during the war.

"Why not?" I replied. I readily accepted everything the Road offered me, no matter how weird and unpredictable it may seem.

Honestly, I didn't feel like going to Čavoglave. I didn't feel like going to the Thompson concert to be in a crowd of 100,000 people. I didn't feel like celebrating Victory Day. Still, when I was in Amsterdam I didn't feel like drinking Coke...

If I ever get a tattoo, I'm going to have a Croatian flag, Madonna and the church of Široki Brijeg, right on my heart – I remembered the idea I got a couple of years before. In those days I used to listen to Thompson, go to church regularly, feel national pride by shouting insults at Dinamo matches. I'd even ended a nine-month relationship because my girlfriend back in those days wasn't sad enough when one Croatian general was arrested.

"We're too different," I'd said to her.

"We're too different," I said to myself, observing the driver who would've definitely approved of my reasons for breaking up with the girl-friend.

How was it possible that I've changed so much in a couple of years? What was the reason?

When I started going to university, I moved with my parents to the suburbs of Zagreb and after eighteen long years got my own room. My freedom. I had my own computer and a fast Internet connection, and since I'd only recently ended a relationship that was everything to me, and since during the first years I rarely went to lessons, I had plenty of time for surfing. Curious as I am, I peeked at every page I came across: I read forums, watched documentaries, studied differ-ent topics. The one thing that made Internet so different from other sources of information was the fact that I could read about a subject from different sources; I had access to different perspectives, a great variety among them.

I didn't have many opportunities to do that before. Church, school and family mainly supported the same ideas. You couldn't go against them because no one ever told you anything that opposed those ideas. You knew that the family was sacred, you knew that your homeland was the best (especially if you grew up in the early nineties when the war was going on) and you knew the flow of history – it was described in school books. You knew that your religion was the best and that if you'd ever experimented with different religions you would end up in hell.

Things weren't like that online. The representatives of both sides were pretty much alike. You could find extreme examples on both sides; you could easily study the arguments and judge who you found more convincing and choose your side.

That was where I perfected the theory. I still kept on going to the church, but I listened carefully to the words of priests, finding several faults and many things to disagree with. I kept on listening to stories about Croatian history and politics during Sunday family lunches, but now I was more informed and knew how to ask awkward questions to which nobody knew the answers.

I started dealing with other theories, although this was only the theoretical side of things. Apart from the people from the virtual world with whom I would exchange a few sentences, I didn't know a person in real life who lived life differently, who talked about different things, a person with a different attitude and lifestyle.

Not until I met Nina, when I was in my third year of university.

"Why do you go to church?" she asked me curiously one Saturday afternoon.

"I don't know..." I tried to come up with an answer. "In my family, going to church is a tradition. I go there to find some kind of peace, a conversation with God, with myself..."

"So, have you ever found peace and talked to God and with yourself during the service?" She wouldn't stop asking.

"Well, maybe the last one," I confessed, "I'm bored quite often so I start talking to myself about all sorts of things."

"Couldn't you do that somewhere else?"

I didn't like her questions. They were forcing me to think about notions that I'd never thought about. I felt stupid when I wasn't able to give her normal answers to the most natural questions.

"I guess I could..." I shrugged.

The following day she accompanied me to Mass.

"Do you agree with this priest when he says that homosexuality is a disease?" she whispered to me during a somewhat homophobic sermon.

"Not really," I replied even more quietly.

"So why don't you say something to him?" She was smiling inconspicuously.

"The things he says are his business, and it's up to me to agree or disagree," I continued, "but I seriously doubt that any kind of a discussion with a priest in the middle of a service would change anything, but only create chaos."

"Whatever you say," now she was the one shrugging, "but it seems to me that by simply being here and not reacting you're supporting him, you're justifying him. You're part of his crew. That's it."

I kept thinking about her words during the rest of the service. Was I truly supporting the priest when he said stuff like that? Was my being there and not reacting a signal of silent approval? Was I defending the Church's sins from the past and all the accusations it's been dealing with lately? Was I approving of and encouraging these actions by throwing a few coins into the church piggy bank every Sunday?

I'd never thought about it like that. Maybe it was time to start.

"And why do you go to football matches?" she asked me not long after we went to church together.

"Because I love my club, the energy on the stands, the sense of pride when we contribute to the victory," I replied instantly.

The following Saturday she was next to me at Maksimir stadium.

"Why do you want to kill the guy who is lying on the field?" she asked me after a foul that made everyone in the stands treat an opponent to shouts involving killing, gallows, Serbians and usual stuff like that.

"Oh, we don't mean it for real" – I was justifying the entire stand – "it's all a part of the folklore. It's part of the fun; the aim is to provoke the guest team. Nobody would *actually* kill him."

"And what if his parents are in the other stand?" she asked me sadly, "how do you think they would feel when a couple of thousand football fans shout these things? Do you think that these ten-year-olds standing next to us, with cigarettes in their mouths, realize that it is all a part of the folklore? Are you sure that one of them won't take it too literally and one day do something serious to someone, just because that someone supports another football club?"

I was looking at her and absorbing her words. I put myself in the shoes of the player who was being carried off the pitch, in the shoes of his parents, in the shoes of the kids from the north stands, in the shoes of everyone who was there listening to the words of hatred. The words of hatred masked in folklore, thus, partially justified.

I kept on going to the matches, but I didn't sing the songs inviting acts of hatred, or provoking the supporters of the other team in any other way. I cheered on my own team and let the others be.

Nina was my muse when it came to observing life in another light. She taught me to reconsider things instead of simply taking similar experiences from the past and applying them to present situations. She taught me that it was okay to have a different opinion from the people who surround you, despite the fact that they may not accept you. It was okay not to be accepted, in fact, sometimes it was even a very welcome characteristic.

Nina was a great teacher and a great friend. Still, she was the only one. Very often, when I wasn't with her, I caught myself thinking if she was, actually, an exception. Was she different from everyone else, interesting, but, consequently, untenable? Can a person like her function in this world leading a normal life? Can a person live outside the system and not be condemned to failure?

And, more importantly, can I?

After all the lessons Nina taught me, I met many CouchSurfers.

Nina wasn't the only one anymore.

Most of the people my roommate and I hosted in our apartment only confirmed that it really was okay to be different, think differently and live differently. They also made me realize that the path wasn't that easy, oh no, but it was worthwhile.

So, after a couple of years, I found myself in Čavoglave. I wasn't right-wing anymore, I wasn't much of a fan of songs with a strong national impulse anymore, I didn't go to Sunday Mass anymore, but the most important thing at that moment was that I wasn't judging those people who still were everything that I no longer was. Why should I? Just because I'd made certain realizations was I above others? The others were less worthy than me, narrow-minded, stupid? Not at all. They were just – dif ferent. If I wanted the others to respect my diversity, I had to do the same thing and respect theirs.

"Do you believe in God?" a fourteen-year-old girl asked me, after I ate a few pieces of dead lamb and splashed it all down with beer, in the company of her brother, her father, and my driver. I guess my outfit, my haircut and my way of traveling made her ask me that.

I avoided her question cunningly, taken aback by the directness of a teenage girl. I started quibbling about the difference between faith and religion, about each and every person being connected in one way or another, but by the look in her eyes I could tell that she didn't understand what I was babbling about. Finally, I just laughed and confessed innocently that I didn't have a simple answer to her question. I told her that we could talk about it some other day, in some other place, in different circumstances.

She wasn't satisfied with that answer.

As much as I wasn't satisfied with her question.

After the end of the concert, with the help of my driver, I ended up on the island of Pag. Since we arrived there in the middle of the night, I had to manage with the accommodation. A part of me was hoping that the good driver would offer me a place to spend the night and carry on my journey the following day, but he'd already done enough for me.

After a bit of snooping around, I found a secluded spot in a bush nearby where I spent the night in a sleeping bag. That was my first wild camp.

The next day, after spending a day on the beach, I felt like going to the mainland. I got onto a ferry and took a look at the map of Croatia. I could've gone home, but I knew it was already late and that I wouldn't make it. I don't like hitchhiking in the dark. Where could I spend the night on my way to Zagreb?

In Senj.

My best friend from high school used to spend his summer vacations in Senj. I hadn't talked to him in years, but I had his phone number somewhere.

Hey, dude! I'm hitchhiking around Croatia, I'm in Senj tonight. I know that the odds of you being there are small, but if you are, call me!

I was the first one to leave the ferry, I dropped my backpack so that everyone could see me and with a wide smile on my face and with my thumb stuck out I started looking for a ride, at least to the highway, because I knew that the road leading to it was steep, long, and winding.

The cars were passing by, one after another. The drivers were smiling and waving at me. Until all of them were gone.

Since I had no idea when the next ferry arrived, I didn't have much choice but put my backpack on and head off slowly feeling a bit disappointed and bummed out.

I was followed by a sunset: it was wonderful to see that the sun was still by my side; however, it wasn't wonderful when I realized that I would arrive at the highway just after sunset, that I would have to find at least one ride before I got to the next town and the fact that I didn't have a place to stay overnight. I'd spent the previous evening in the bushes, would I have to do the same thing that night?

At that moment I received a message.

I've just arrived to Senj. Let me know once you're here.

I jumped a little bit, laughed from the bottom of my heart, looked at the sky and said: Thank you, God.

Wait a minute. God? Only yesterday a girl asked me whether I believed in Him, and I didn't know what to say to her, and now I was suddenly thanking Him. So, do I believe in Him or not?

The fact was that during the past couple of years we'd drifted apart a bit: I'd been following my own path, with my own rules, not the rules of the Church. I got bored with the Church, I didn't find what the priests were preaching interesting anymore, and some of them said things that made me want to leave the church out of pure protest. All I could see in it all was mass brainwashing of people who didn't feel like using their own brains.

However, after I'd given it a thought, I realized that I held grudges against the Church as an institution and some priests, not against God. I still thanked Him spontaneously in the moments of happiness. Should I work on our relationship: sort it out once and for all?

Okay. Let's go. I had plenty of time.

I was treading slowly with a heavy backpack on my back, every once in a while throwing a quick glance at the sunset. I started the conversation.

"Hi, God," I said.

"Hello, Tomislav," I replied to myself using a deeper voice, and since God is all-powerful and controls everything, I guess He was the one to put these words in my mouth.

"I know I haven't talked to you in years, and I used to do that," I continued "mostly before I went to sleep or when I needed something. It probably wasn't a very nice thing for me to do, but I'm sure you've forgiven me. Let's go and sort some things out. You can see it as my confession because I really don't feel like going into a small, dark little confessional in a church to confess my sins to a priest, sins that I don't repent for and that I keep on repeating. So, we're doing it like this, without a middleman. In order for us not to get lost, let us take the Ten Commandments you've given to humankind and talk about them for a bit."

1. I am the Lord your God, you shall have no other gods before me

"So, what's up with this one, feeling a little jealous? Only kidding. Yes, I understand this commandment. Speaking of which, may we refer to them with some other term? I have certain problems with the word 'commandment'. Can I call them 'suggestions'?"

"Yes, you can."

"Thank you. So, this suggestion makes perfect sense, if we refer to the fact that we shouldn't worship other, fake gods, like, let's say, money. I don't believe that you'd be jealous if some people were to worship other gods just because they were born in other parts of the world, would you? All gods have similar attitudes when it comes to certain things. I am somehow convinced that this was your intention when you handed the suggestions to the people: we shouldn't go looking for comfort and sense in superficial things because that won't lead us anywhere. There, I promise that I'll do my best to follow only important things in my life, and not to be led astray by twaddle. Okay?"

"Okay."

"Great, a man can arrange everything with you."

2. Do not take the name of the Lord in vain

"You mean, You don't want me to curse You? Well, I guess it makes sense. It's pure logic. If I believe in You, I have no reason to curse You because I should be convinced that you're doing everything in the best way possible and for good reasons (after all, if Your own Son didn't curse you after everything you put Him through...). And, if I don't believe in You, why should I mention You? So, I promise that I won't be cursing You, just like I never have. That one time when I got into a fight in the seventh grade and cursed You trying to insult the boy who cut my lip, yeah, sorry for that."

"Okay," he replied politely.

3. Remember the Sabbath and keep it holy

"You mean, I should go to church on Sundays? Well, I cannot promise You that for several reasons. First, I find Mass awfully tedious. At least in the church where I go. And, frankly, I really don't want to search for a church and an interesting priest every Sunday. Second, and much more important, I disagree with many things I hear priests preach. For instance, they talk about homosexuality as if it were a disease. They are against contraception. Don't get me started on all the scandals that have shaken the Church for the last couple of years – and the Church hasn't responded very firmly to that. I know that I could go to church for my own sake, to find inner peace or whatever, but those standing at the altar only distract me from the process. And by participating in Mass I'm giving them my consent and agreeing with them without saying anything. There are many things that I don't agree with, so I believe I would be a hypocrite if I went to Mass every Sunday. I won't even mention the luxury and the waste of money, new cars, palaces, and God knows what."

"If by this commandment, that is, suggestion, you were referring to the idea that you don't have to actually go to church one day a week, but instead dedicate one day a week to worshiping You, no problem. Hey, if one is not enough, I will celebrate You every single day, in my own way: I will lead my life as I consider it right, following my conscience – the very same conscience You've given me. I think it should guide me well."

4. Honour your father and mother

"I have nothing to add to this one, they deserve it. I don't know how I'd feel if I'd had bad parents who'd abused me in my youth, but having the best parents in the world, I really don't have anything to add. There, I promise to respect my parents, more than ever before. A person learns how to appreciate his or her parents when they leave their home. Also, soon I'll stop lying to them about my travelling habits. I'm only doing it for their sake. Okay?"

"Okay."

5. You shall not kill

"Really? Well, if you hadn't suggested this I would never have thought of it myself. But, okay, I shall not kill. However, you haven't been quite clear about it. What about killing animals? Does it make it okay if they're killed for food? What about plants? They're living beings, too. Alright, this commandment probably refers to people. But, what if it happens in self-defence? What if someone kills a very bad person and by doing so, he or she saves the lives of other people? What about euthanasia, when people decide that they don't want to live for years as vegetables? What about abortion, when a child has a slim chance of surviving, and the pregnancy can put the mother's life in danger? Those are the things that should be straightened out, but I understand they're not easy to discuss so I'll leave them for some other time, if necessary. I hope it won't be."

6. You shall not commit adultery

"Well, this one's interesting. What does it even mean? When I was younger I know that it meant that if I masturbate I will have to confess what I've done. Because it is a sin. Really, God? And the whole no sex before marriage policy? Oh, come on. Please? I mean, I agree that you shouldn't get involved in 'fornicating' when someone can get hurt, or when you only want to satisfy your own needs without taking into consideration the feelings of the other person. However, the only way I could get hurt by masturbating is if I think, during the whole act, about having to go and confess my sin. Also, I'm not that excited about the whole 'you shouldn't have sex before marriage' thing. Sexuality is a taboo. Why? You've given it to us and made it wonderful, but you've forbidden it at the same time. It doesn't make sense. But okay, let's do it this way. I promise I won't enter into relationship to satisfy my needs and sexual appetites, especially if there is a possibility of the other person getting hurt. There, I can do that. I can be honest. I'm able not to hurt women, not to lie to them, not to trick them just so I can satisfy my needs."

7. You shall not steal

"This one is easy. Okay, I won't. Generally speaking, I won't do unto others what I don't want others to do unto me."

8. You shall not bear false witness against your neighbour

"By and large, I agree. Still, some things could and maybe should be left unsaid, for everyone's sake. For example, not admitting to my parents that I'm hitchhiking. It would only make my Mom worry about me. Also, when I'm travelling and I come down with something I will always say to her that I'm great. And if that means bearing false witnesses, well fuck it, I'll keep on doing it. However, if someone bears false witnesses only to do harm to others and good to themselves, then I agree with You and I promise that I'll try to stop doing it."

9. You shall not covet your neighbour's wife

"Okay, I'll do my best not to get involved with someone else's wife. Still, what do you think about those people who remain married even though they're unhappy? In my opinion, it is better to end a marriage in which there's no love and look for someone else than suffer for years and involve other innocent people in that suffering. What if I met a woman who is filing for divorce, but due to administration issues she still cannot get a divorce? Once again, there are many things to straighten out. But okay, I get it the point, there wasn't much space on Moses' stone tablets. I'll do my best not to break someone's marriage or relationship, unless I judge it's the best for all parties involved."

10. You shall not covet anything that belongs to your neighbour

"You shall not covet, you shall not covet. There is nothing bad if every once in a while you have a bad or negative thought; it's important that you discard them and not react to them. You should not let them come to the surface. I mean, if I simply covet something that belongs to someone else, I'm not harming anyone. However, if a simple wish becomes an act, then we should go back to the sixth commandment."

"There we go, God, I arrived at the highway talking to You. And I really had a nice time. I'm glad we've cleared up the things that we didn't manage to deal with before. The most important thing I learned, the only thing that matters, the thing You've given to me from the very start, is my conscience. I will listen to it as much as I can."
"And now I'm off hitchhiking."
"Go in peace," He concluded.
As an award for the conversation God sent me a car in less than five minutes: just enough time to change my sweaty T-shirt. Loud music was blaring from the car, heavy metal or something like that, I could never tell one genre from others that include so much electric guitar and screaming. Two guys, who were a bit (too) happy and dressed all in black, were sitting in the front, and a huge black dog was lying on the back seat.
"Hmm", I thought, stopping for a moment, "screaming from the radio, two guys dressed in black and a black dog. Maybe God didn't send this car, perhaps the other one did..."
"There is no other one, you fool." I heard the same deep voice from

within. "The other was made up only to scare those of little faith. Fear is the best means of control. The Church knows its job; they've been using it for ages. Also, look, these two have rosemary hanging from their rear-view mirror."

He was right. I shouldn't judge people by screaming from the radio, black clothes and black dog. Also, I shouldn't judge them by the rosemary. I got in, patted the dog and introduced myself to my new friends.

They were drunk on *gemišt*[12]. They politely offered me some, and I politely accepted.

"I thought we sorted out everything with our conversation, and now You're trying to kill me?" I carried on my monologue from before. "How rude."

"God works in mysterious ways," he replied sarcastically, "but, hey, at least I gave you something to drink before you die."

"Very funny," I concluded our conversation and took a sip.

The driver was driving slowly, but he was pretty insecure behind the wheel. And the road: one curve after another. By applying the theory of relativity, only fifty kilometres to Senj became too many kilometres ahead of us. Cars were piling up behind us. The screaming from the radio continued, my new friends were singing along loudly, while the dog and I simply exchanged looks on the back seat wondering when we would arrive at our destination. And if we would arrive alive.

"Cops!" One of the guys shouted to the other, noticing the cops two hundred metres from us. I was sure that they would pull us over, we were at the beginning of the caravan and we were zigzagging even though we didn't exceed the speed limit.

However, just when we'd noticed them, a nervous driver behind us decided to overtake us, crossing a solid white line. The cops saw it, of course, and made him pull over. An impatient guy, without even knowing it, saved us.

I arrived in Senj safe and sound, met my friend, spent the night at his place, and the following day returned to Zagreb.

Once again, just as after I came from Sofia, I was lying on my couch wondering how it was possible for so many things to happen in only one week on the road. However, the only difference was that I wasn't thinking about paying my debts, finishing the university and travelling the world.

I had other things on my mind.

---

[12] A drink made of wine mixed with sparkling water.

Day 794.

Everything was happening so fast during those days: I wasn't thinking, planning, or weighing up the possible consequences of the decisions I was taking. It was as if an inner voice, my gut maybe, was telling me to go on; to listen to it.

The only one disagreeing with it all, the only opponent, the only party pooper was another voice within me. Fear. It was convincing me that I couldn't face the challenge, that so many things could go wrong and that it was safer to remain in the known environment. It was telling me that I shouldn't take risks.

My instinct was against my fear. Two inner voices hiding deep down within me, diametrically opposed to each other and easily interchangeable.

I realized that if instinct and fear were diametrically opposed, every human being, by their nature, is instinctively brave. The curiosity, the need to discover new places, the wish to meet new people, making new realizations, all those characteristics come naturally to people. Our being is longing for the new, the unexplored, the hidden. It fulfils us, makes us happy, gives sense to our lives.

Fear is, on the other hand, an acquired feeling that sneaks up inconspicuously on our minds, from the very beginning of our life, working through education and our environment. Our entire society can be defined as a society of fear. Fear is everywhere: fear of failure at school, at work, in love. Fear of not being accepted by one's family, friends, lovers. Fear of being judged by your parents, bosses, partners.

Our entire society is a society of adaptation: adaptation to one group of people, to another group, and so on. Adaptation in order not to be afraid anymore; and to lull ourselves into the false feeling of security. A security that is superfluous to instinct.

In fact, life boils down to a constant struggle between those two forces. Once our nature beats the unnatural fear – that will be it. We will set the basis for the future struggles.

During those days my instinct had fear on the ropes.

"Soon after I finished my tour around Croatia," I continued with my conversation with Daniela, "I totally lost it, I moved out, quit my job, left my stuff at my parents' place and embarked on my longest journey – a two-month hitchhiking tour around Europe."

Day 278.

"See you soon," she told me the following morning as we were saying goodbye in front of her building.

She gave me the most sincere smile she was capable of making, turned around and walked away. I did the same thing, after a short break. I left, but in the other direction. I didn't turn around. And I was sure she didn't turn around either.

As I was walking down some big avenue in Berlin, it crossed my mind that I could go back home and take up where I'd left my exams and job. However, it would only mean that I accepted defeat, that I embraced giving up and that I was returning to my old life. My old life – the one I didn't like. The one I got away from. The one I ran away from.

I looked up to the sky, searching for an answer. The sun was looking at me. It was shining brightly. It hadn't changed since I started my journey. It will continue to shine in the same way, no matter how many thick clouds want to cover its brightness; it will continue to shine despite the fact it hides itself for a few hours every day. Nobody can do anything to it. It just continues to rock away, despite everything and everyone.

I will look up to it – I thought – I will put a smile on my face and move on. Straight away. There was no time, need or use for being sad, disappointed or looking to past events with nostalgia. You are where you are. It is only up to you to make the most of it. Don't turn around. Time to go.

I stood in the middle of the road, took the map out of my backpack and chose the direction – west. In an Internet café I sent a last-minute request for a couch in Hamburg, and checked the easiest way to get out of Berlin and arrived on the highway so I could start hitchhiking again.

The adventure was on.

An hour and a half later, after a short ride in a train, finding my way through a thick forest, using a compass to orientate myself and crossing a bridge, I finally arrived at a gas station outside Berlin and was talking to drivers who could give me a ride. In the meanwhile, I received a message from a CouchSurfer from Hamburg. I had a place to stay for the next few days.

"What do you do?" I stared a conversation with the driver, who, after a few people that replied *Nein*, said *Ja*. He was driving a sand coloured van with black lines on it that was falling apart: it was almost the same vehicle as that of serial killers you see in American movies.

"Currently, I'm living with my daughter on an estate between Berlin and Hamburg," he said with a hoarse voice and with a strong accent by which I couldn't define where he was from. "I'm a dog trainer, but very often people come to me to go through military training."

"Military training?" I was confused.

"Yes, military training," he carried on lighting a cigarette, "surviving in the wilderness, conditioning, handling weapons and stuff like that."

"I see," I said quietly thanking God that we were in the middle of a highway so he couldn't drag me to his training centre.

"I worked for many years in Ireland," – that's where he got his accent. "I was a mercenary for the IRA, so I have quite a lot of experience in that area. I still feel most comfortable behind the sniper scope. That is my natural position."

I listened to him, silently watching him exhaling the cigarette smoke and talking nonchalantly about murdering people for money, back in Ireland. In cold blood. I had to use a special *bullshit filter* in order to tell whether he was making it all up or not. The result was negative. I was driving with a hit man. Moreover, I was in a van that looked like the vans of serial killers in American movies.

"I was very good at what I did," he continued, knowing that he'd left me speechless, "if I hadn't done it, someone else would've." He was justifying his actions. "Besides, I thought I was fighting for the right cause."

He started talking about the political situation in Ireland, justifying murder for "the greater cause", and after half an hour I had to admit that everything he'd said actually made sense. The man sitting next to me was actually quite a nice person.

After a few years of active service he didn't want to fight anymore, his daughter was born and he moved to the country. He found peace there, he said to me. At one moment I caught myself thinking that I would actually like him to invite me to spend a night or two at his place, but that didn't happen. Maybe it was better that way because I couldn't guarantee how he'd react if I liked his 17-year-old daughter.

He left me on a gas station and two rides later I arrived to Hamburg along with the night. I went to the house of my host Johann.

As I climbed up the stairs I sensed wonderful aromas of something cooking coming from one of the apartments, something that I would obviously associate with my Berlin uplift. I was hoping it would be coming from Johann's apartment.

And it was.

A tall and handsome guy with a wide smile on his face and holding a bottle of beer opened the door.

"You're just about in time for dinner," he said, hugging me.

I love hugs. In fact, it is the unofficial salute among CouchSurfers: warm, friendly, intimate. Instant connection, breaking the walls that can be quite an obstacle when you start building a relationship between two people.

I was slowly getting to know my host over the spiciest, and maybe even the most delicious dinner I'd ever had, and an unlimited amount of beer. He was forty and living with his partner, who was currently out of town, and that was the reason why he could host people. He was a jolly fellow living in what could easily be the most beautiful apartment I'd ever been in. Everything was so spotless. They took care of the smallest details, the towels in the bathroom were so neatly folded that even my Mom would be jealous, and when you opened the bathroom door a light would turn on instantly and classical music would start to play from a small radio player.

"When was the first time you realized you were gay?" I asked him naturally, after a few beers, excited that I could finally talk openly to someone about those things. I knew a couple of people in Zagreb who were gay, but I wasn't close to any one of them so I couldn't talk freely about that topic, which was, at least where I'm from, still taboo.

"Believe it or not, when I was very young, when I was four or five years old," he replied in an even more natural way. "I was in the hospital to have my tonsils taken out and I distinctly remember one boy I couldn't stay away from. Of course, back then I was too young to understand my feelings, but as the years passed I realized that it was a part of me from birth. I did try something with girls as a teenager, but I soon realized that there was no point: I didn't feel anything when I was with them, despite their appearance."

"And how did your family and friends react?" I asked him, sipping my beer and imagining what my parents would say if told them that I was spending the night in the company of a forty-year-old homosexual, in his apartment, with a lot of alcohol. And not only my parents, how would my friends react if I told them that, as it happens, I liked guys?

"They were totally cool about it," he said. "I believe the secret lies in the fact that they'd known several people with the same affinities, which helped them convince themselves that they were completely normal people who just happen to have different habits, aspirations and life-styles. Naturally, I've lost some friends, but I don't regret it. Do I even need friends who cannot accept me for who I am?"

My new friend was speaking wisely.

The following morning a large glass of water was waiting for me by the headboard, perfect to help prevent a hangover. As I wasn't really able to remember everything that had happened the previous night (!) I wasn't quite sure how the glass found its way to me, as if I'd ordered it.

"What is this glass of water doing here?" I asked Johann as I heard the rattle of dishes in the kitchen.

"I brought it to you this morning, we had a lot to drink last night, so..." He replied as he was leaving the kitchen carrying a tray with a couple of small sandwiches with cheese and jam.

My first breakfast in bed.

"Johann, your are the king of hospitality," I said munching, "I wouldn't mind a bit if I had a girlfriend like you."

He chuckled, sat next to me and helped me with the rest of the delicious sandwiches.

We spent the following few days together, cycling the streets of Hamburg, having lunch with his colleagues, swimming at the sandy beach placed next to the third most active harbour in Europe, enjoying movies laid back on a big marital bed. If I ever showed any signs of homophobia it was completely finished off by spending a few days in the company of that sweet homosexual.

That could be the best way of curing homophobia, racism and religious intolerance: put two different people in the same room and let them hang out. Once they realize that the other, no matter how different, is basically the same, the prejudices will collapse like a house of cards.

As my stay in Hamburg was coming to an end I had to take out my map of Europe and pick my next direction. Where should I go? I'd arrived from the east; there was nothing interesting on the south, so maybe north? Or should I go on westward?

I studied CS profiles in Copenhagen and sent a mail to an interesting guy. I stressed that I would be coming only if he could host me, if not, I would be going in the other direction.

I received a reply in a matter of few minutes. And the reply was negative. I threw another quick glance at the map and made one of the easiest decisions ever: Amsterdam, here I come.

Day 283.

"Hello," I greeted a guy in a suit and tie as he was entering his SUV, somewhere near Hannover. Even though my earlier experience with people in expensive cars was telling me that the chances of him giving me a ride were slim, I had nothing to lose. I never have anything to lose. Besides, he was the only one at the gas station with Dutch licence plates.

"Hello," he greeted me back cautiously.

"Do you happen to be headed for the Netherlands?" I was smiling and glancing at his plates making it clear to him that it was quite obvious where he was heading.

"Yes, I am," he continued with the same caution as before, "why?"

"Well, you know," I started, "I've been hitchhiking across Europe for a couple of weeks now, I don't have much money and I'm headed for Amsterdam so I was wondering if you could give me a ride for at least one part of the route."

"Where are you from?"

"From Croatia."

"Will you kill me I give you a ride?"

"Will you kill me?"

"No."

"Okay, then I won't kill you either."

Humour always worked. He gave me another look and that was it: I got into the car.

It was one of the most interesting, fastest and most comfortable rides ever. In two hours, which was the time the ride lasted, we touched upon various subjects, the conversation flowing easily. He told how he, in a similar way, travelled when he was my age, and now he had a factory with seventy workers, a son studying in the USA, a wife he still adored and so on. He was a very pleasant, intelligent and interesting person.

"Thank you very much," I said as I was taking my backpack out of the trunk some eighty kilometres from Amsterdam. I was only one ride, or maybe two, away from my destination for the day.

"Oh, you're welcome," he replied sincerely, grabbing his back pocket, "here, that's for you."

There was, just like that suitcase in *Pulp Fiction*, a fifty Euro bill shining in his hand.

"Thank you, but I really cannot accept it." I refused his offer still feeling a bit hypnotised.

"Why?" he wanted to know.

"Why?" I was taken aback. "You've already done me a huge favour by giving me a ride for a good part of the way: it is only because of you that I will be in Amsterdam before dark. And now you still want me to take money from you. That wouldn't be fair."

"Let me explain it to you," he began, "these fifty Euros don't mean much to me and they could to you. You're travelling across Europe, you don't have much money, and this could help you a bit. I know because I travelled the same way."

"But..."

"There is no but," he insisted, "I won't take no for an answer. In fact, you'll be doing me a favour if you take it. It would make me feel better if I knew I'd helped someone today. So, we both win."

He made a good point. These fifty Euros could come in handy, and it won't harm him if he's left without. Moreover, he will feel better. I took the bill, thanking him once again from the bottom of my heart, pranced a bit as I watched him leave the gas station. I was rich!

I calculated quickly that with that donation my daily expenses dropped to less than five Euros a day. Now I just had to keep them that low...

In less than a couple of minutes I understood why the Netherlands was popular in hitchhiking circles. I had already managed to find my last ride to Amsterdam. My driver was a jolly British guy.

"Where are you from?" he asked me.

"From Croatia," I replied politely, fastening my seat belt.

"Croatia?" he frowned, "yes, yes, there are many sea cucumbers there, aren't there?"

Déjà vu. Where had I heard the story before, that when a person hears about Croatia, of all things it's known for, the first thing that comes to their mind is squalid sea cucumbers.

Ha, I got it.

"A couple of months ago was hitchhiking around Croatia and a nice man from Hungary gave me a ride," I began. "He told me a story about a sea cucumber business; how he and his partner intended to export them to the Japanese market where they are considered an exquisite treat since they are rich in protein. At first, I didn't believe him, but he had quite a detailed business plan so I even left him my e-mail address in case he needed a sea cucumber picker. It would definitely be a cool occupation, and well paid."

The Brit was listening to me carefully and gave me an incredulous look from time to time.

"From Hungary?" he asked me after a brief silence, "do you remember his name?"

"His name?" I repeated, "I have no idea, we spent an half an hour together and I never heard from him again."

He was silent again. He took out his cell phone, dialled a number and put the phone to his ear.

"Hey, partner," he started the conversation with the person on the other end of the phone, "did you, by any chance, pick up a hitchhiker a few months ago in Croatia and talk to him about our sea cucumber business? You did? I have too, a few kilometres from Amsterdam."

He handed me his phone, smiling showily. On the other end was the man who, a few months ago, gave me a ride to Zadar. We exchanged a few sentences, not believing that we were actually talking to each other: what were the odds?

Unfuckingbelievable.

I loved my new life, just like I loved the town I was arriving in. I adored it.

I adored everything about it: its inhabitants who always wore a wide smile on their faces as they were riding their colourful bikes; its street lights that said how many seconds you had until the green light came on; its squeaking trams honking every now and then to let people know they were arriving. I adored its circular streets bordered by canals where you could see someone's floating home, connected by numberless bridges, where I'd gotten lost so many times, but never cared. I adored its neighbourhoods in which behind every corner you could expect the intoxicating scent of a plant that was prohibited anywhere else, or you could expect a woman in her underwear inviting you to spend some intimate time with her for only a couple of tens of Euros. I adored its street artists: jugglers, musicians, beggars – all of them make you feel as if you are in a giant open air theatre – a city where something is always happening. I adored its unique bricked houses, tossed around in all directions. I adored its museums, which even I, with my professional couldn't-care-less-about-art attitude, enjoyed. I adored its parks, and particularly Vondelpark, which, on a sunny day, was a gathering place for families and friends to play soccer or badminton, and in the evening you could see people dressed as stuffed animals running around or men in suits saluting to each other and doing push-ups.

I adored the grey clouds above it; I adored its frustrating rain and the unstopping wind. I adored its streets early in the morning, empty and still dirty from the previous night's parties, full of broken bottles and food remains. I adored its famous coffee shops, where in a claustrophobic atmosphere you could hear giggling, deep conversations about the meaning of life, and nonchalant assistance of the waiters to guests who, due to excessive consumption of weed, suddenly went pale and dropped their heads on the table. I adored its Red Light District, cocaine dealers, prostitutes with empty eyes and drunk passers-by who appeared never to have seen a naked woman. I adored its numerous tourists who came there with one intention only: not to remember anything when they left a couple of days later.

I adored the people I ran into every time I got there.

"Maaike, nice to meet you," my new host welcomed me with a hug to her cute one-room apartment near the centre of the city, which she shared with her dog Lola and four nameless puppies.

"Make yourself at home, I know that you've had an exhausting day so if you want to take a shower feel free. I'm going to prepare us something to eat."

I accepted her offer whole-heartedly and shortly after I was washing six hundred kilometres off of my body.

"Hey, there is nothing better than having a warm shower after a whole day spent hitchhiking," I exclaimed enthusiastically as I exited the bathroom with a towel wrapped around my hips.

"Are you sure?" she asked approaching with a tray with two giant sandwiches, a glass of red wine and a famous Amsterdam specialty, a joint that was a mix of tobacco and *White Widow*.

"Well, girl, you really know how to please a man," I said happily and only later realising what I'd said.

"Oh, it's nothing," she readily accepted the play on words winking at me and throwing a quick glance on my half-naked body.

I had a feeling that we would get along quite well.

After I made myself decent, I dug into the food listening to her, only superficially focusing my attention on one thing that was truly interesting to me – her face. She was beautiful, but her face was drained by a lack of kilograms, and she was very pale. She had long, straight brown hair, a shy smile and direct green eyes.

She appeared to be brave. She didn't hesitate to make direct eye contact, or talk about delicate subjects. Very often she would start talking about sex as if she wanted to make it clear that she was open-minded, careless and unreachable. But at the same time, she was timid – I had a feeling that by talking so directly she was, in fact, unconsciously defending herself from something much simpler, more ordinary and more natural. It seemed to me that she was defending herself from talking about topics against which she wasn't protected by shocking words and her collocutors' visualizations; from topics where, rather than talking about baring her body, she would be made to bare her mind to others.

"I'm thinking about getting myself a slave," she said all of a sudden, looking straight at me.

"A what?" I coughed, ruining a particularly good pull on the intoxicating smoke.

"A slave," she smiled innocently, "there are people who enjoy that, and I could really use one."

"And how does that work exactly?" I inhaled carefully, making up for the last lost toke and paid close attention to what she was saying.

"It's very simple," she started, "you place an ad online in which you say that you're looking for a slave. There are even pages specializing in that kind of thing. And then people who're interested in your ad contact you. I don't have first-hand experience since I placed my ad only recently."

"What did you write?" I couldn't believe my ears.

"I wrote that men were worthless to me. Women are the ones who make things happen. They are smarter, more beautiful, more sociable, better in what they do, more communicative and they are the creators of life. We don't even need men to get us pregnant anymore. All this means that men are here to serve us" she laughed proudly and spitefully. "The person who accepts to be my slave has to take care that my apartment is always spotless, do my groceries, walk my dog, cook dinner, paint my walls, everything I may need. If I want an orgasm, he will have to satisfy me in the way I please without looking me directly in the eyes. If I don't want to see his face, I will put him in the closet. He will have to give me all of his money and his credit card pin numbers. I will give him a weekly allowance which would suffice for his basic needs and the rest of it will be mine."

"And?" I still couldn't believe it.

"You're not going to believe it," she was reading my mind, "but one guy said yes. He told me his exact salary, 1800 Euros a month and after he pays for food, his apartment and monthly expenses he has 900 Euros left.

It would be so easy to save the money for journeys," she smiled.

"Yeah right." I observed her, realizing that she wasn't messing with me. "How can you tell that you're not dealing with a crazy person?" I asked her, remembering instantly that I'd hosted hundreds of people in my apartment over the past few years, via CS, in the same way. I'd also arrived at her apartment in the same way, after we exchanged only one e-mail.

"It's all in the eyes," she said giving me once again an intense look, "trust me, if I have learnt anything in my life, then that is knowing what kind of person I'm dealing with. I can tell from a mile who's dangerous and who's not. I can tell whether a person is neurotic, psychotic, a pathological liar and stuff like that. It's all in the eyes. The guy who'd contacted me isn't dangerous. He is gentle with slightly strange tastes. His mother must've been a dominant figure and she might've abused him. I don't know the exact reason but I can guess it."

While she was saying the last words she lowered her eyes. She realized that her eyes might tell a lot of things too. And that wasn't her plan.

Day 291.

After a few days in Amsterdam the road took me to Utrecht, Gent and, finally, to Lille where I stayed at my friend Thomas's place.

Thomas was one of the main reasons why I travel today: he was the one who showed me the magic of CouchSurfing. A couple of years before, just as I left my parents' home I bumped into him in the centre of Zagreb with a French flag and a couple of bags hanging from a cool bike. He explained to me that he was travelling across Europe as a part of a university project and that he was looking for a place to spend the night in his tent without getting his bike or his kidney stolen.

Since my roommate and I had free space on the floor of our rented apartment I invited him to crash at our place.

Over a couple of beers, he told us that there was a web page created for hospitable people like us and that he had used it a couple of times on his Journey. The page was – CouchSurfing.

"Things are still in their infancy," he said, "there aren't many registered members, but the number of members keeps on growing from one day to another."

That night he helped me set up my profile and left me my first positive reference. That was how it started. Later on, my first surfing experience in Amsterdam took place; travellers began arriving and staying at our place in Zagreb and, finally, the journey I was on.

The same way we drank Croatian beer and ate Croatian food in Zagreb, now we were drinking French wine and eating *baguettes* and *camembert* going through the numerous events that happened to us over the past few years and exchanging different stories.

"Where are you going after Lille?" he asked me the following day.

"Frankly, I have no idea," I replied, "I didn't plan ending up here either."

I threw a quick glance at the map of Europe and in less than a couple of seconds I knew where to go next.

Paris.

Day 293.

Lille and Paris were 222 kilometres of straight highway apart. For a hitchhiker that was always good news because you could almost always count on a single ride – fast, no changing rides and not too much stress. Almost always. This one, however, was another good day for a hitchhiking lesson: when you hitchhike, don't count on anything.

The first important thing about hitchhiking is to find a good position to leave the town, one where there are cars going in your direction. You should take care that there are plenty of cars, that they have a place to pull over and that they aren't driving too fast, that is, they have enough time to notice you and react. I'd taken care of all these factors. I also had a pretty nice 'PARIS' sign, which was quite straight forward about where I was planning to go that day.

Still, despite these contributing factors, no one would pull over. One hour, two hours, three hours.

Three hours of standing on one place with my thumb stuck out looking all those cars pass by me and not one of them deigning to pull over would easily make you go insane. So you start dancing in order for people to notice you and pay attention, you climb on a small wall and jump off of it improvising all sorts of thumb up choreographies; in the end, you even get down on your knees and start begging for a ride, but still nothing. No use.

At the peak of my madness, I took the sign, flipped it to the other side and with a thick marker pen I wrote a large question mark. Fuck Paris, I would go anywhere just to leave this place.

In less than two minutes after putting my new plan into action a car pulled over. I exclaimed excitedly. I ran quickly to the driver and without asking anything got into the car – drive!

My new friend, a young guy of African origin, didn't go to Paris. He made a stop at the next gas station, took a road map and went to have a word with a truck driver who was having his lunch break just as we got there. He asked him for a piece of an advice, about which road to take in order for him to leave me on a good place to continue my hitchhiking adventure to Paris. After a few minutes of consulting with the truck driver he left me at a gas station a few kilometres away and took off in the opposite direction. We shook hands and exchanged smiles. I was the reason why he'd lost at least half an hour of what could be his precious time, but still he'd decided to give a helping hand to a stranger and do everything he could to assist me.

Five hours and four rides later I was in Paris. The last driver gave me an unused metro ticket so I could find Melissa, a girl I was supposed to stay while I was in the French capital.

Melissa was a CouchSurfer whom I'd met a couple of weeks before, during my stay in Prague. She was staying in the same place I was, along with ten other CouchSurfers.

She was an 18-year-old French girl, originally from Algeria. I was listening to her talking about her life for the past couple of months to those gathered around the table: being broke, on the road, changing cities, friends and jobs. Each end every person around the table was listening to her words attentively, feeling slightly jealous about her lifestyle, which she shared so naturally with the others.

I also paid attention to her words, remembering my own experiences with many CouchSurfers who had passed through my apartment and who'd had experiences similar to hers. I absorbed everything, just as I had absorbed everything back then. So I realized that soon I also would have similar stories to tell because just a couple of days before I had embarked on a similar big adventure.

"So, are you happy?" I whispered in her ear as soon as she stopped talking to the others. Somehow, I'd always imagined someone living like that being truly happy, but now that I was experiencing something similar I was wondering whether happiness came with it, by default. So I decided to check with her.

She needed a moment to come up with an answer. She looked at me directly, as if she was trying to discern something in my eyes.

"I like you," she said self-assuredly, taking her eyes off me and carrying on with her meal, "you're the first person who's asked me this. Everyone is pleased with the mere surface of the adventures they pass through when they live this kind of life. They take it for granted that happiness is part of it all."

"You see, a journey can be a sort of an escape," she continued chewing the delicious dinner prepared by our Swedish host. The menu contained a delicious lentil soup (I stole the recipe later and prepared the same meal for my hosts on the journey), and for dessert he prepared muffins (I even took the recipe for the muffins and credited myself with them for many years to come).

"But the truth is that you cannot escape life. The journey won't solve all of your problems. It is only going to force you to approach those problems from a different perspective – you may happen to solve some of them when you return home. If you do return home, of course."

I thanked her for the answer and for having satisfied my curiosity. So, travelling doesn't necessarily equal happiness.

"If you ever happen to find yourself in Paris, don't be a stranger" she finished and went back to eating.

Twenty days later I actually found myself in Paris, so I decided to contact her. I came to her door.

"Oh, it's you," she opened the door and gave me a hug, "your beard is a bit bigger than the last time I saw you."

"I know, yours too," I replied and entered her home.

She smiled and took me to the room where I was supposed to sleep. She lived with her parents, who were out of town at the moment and who were supposed to come back home the following morning.

"Take a rest, take a shower if you want to and then we're going out" she informed me, "but hurry up, I made some arrangements with a bunch of friends, we're going for a barbecue, you're invited, too, of course."

I was ready in less than half an hour.

"So, what's your story?" I asked her as we were walking down the street, towards the metro station.

"I was born and raised in Algeria where I had a difficult childhood," she started. She was dressed all in black with a white shirt that was a size too large. She had black fishnet socks and black patent-leather heels. She wore glasses. The way she moved radiated a dose of sex appeal that was only accentuated by the way she dressed. She was barely of age, fully conscious of her youth and beauty and she wore it proudly. And, there was also something French about her. "The people I live with aren't my real parents, but my uncle and aunt. We don't get on very well, but they're the only people I have here. However, I've started working recently, so I hope that soon I may have enough money to move out."

"And what do you do?" I asked.

"Hmmm," she observed me closely. "Can I count on your open-mindedness, but also on your capacity to keep a secret? After all, we have many friends in common."

"Sure," I said convincingly while a number of thoughts passed through my head.

"Guess," she decided to play with me.

"Do you work on a hotline?" I blurted out jokingly, but that was my most serious attempt.

"You're close," she winked at me, "just leave the phone part out and that's it."

"Are you being serious?" I looked at her, reminding myself of the promise I'd made earlier on.

"Dead serious."

"You're a prostitute?" I caught myself whispering.

"Not really," she tried to explain, "I'm not some kind of a hooker who can be picked up on a corner and fucked for fifty Euros. I work as an exclusive escort lady and only by recommendation."

"Aren't you afraid?" was the first thing I managed to say, although a handful of other questions crossed my mind.

"I don't live in London at the turn of the 19th century," she laughed.

"Why are you doing it?" I couldn't keep my curiosity hidden. Prejudices and judgment tried to fight their way to the surface, but I managed to push them down and give way to curiosity. You need curiosity in the situations like that one, while prejudice and judgement are totally useless, especially since I planned to travel, listen and learn from people who had completely different lifestyles.

"First, I need the money," she began, "the school fees at the Sorbonne are high. Second, I don't have any problem with sleeping with strangers. After everything that the strangers have done to me as a kid, believe me, there aren't many things I haven't seen before. Third, by satisfying strangers' sexual desires, directly or indirectly, I may be preventing them from looking for someone who wouldn't be that keen on pleasing them. For instance, preventing them from finding a nine-year-old girl in Algeria."

"Fuck," I blurted out, "I'm sorry."

"You shouldn't be," she was talking about all these difficult things so easily, "it wasn't that bad for me."

"What do you mean?"

"When I was eleven I witnessed an eight-year-old girl being raped by three men. I was in the same room. One of the tools they used was a beer bottle. A broken beer bottle."

Suddenly, my mind went blank. I put my palms on my knees feeling nauseated. Melissa came a few steps nearer, chewing the snacks she'd bought a few minutes earlier. She was standing up straight in heels, looking at me so intensely that I could almost see in her eyes the horrible scene that'd made me sick.

"I'm not sure whether I want to hear more stuff like that," I said as soon as I was a bit better.

"You asked, I answered." She was direct. "However, I think that people should be aware of what's going on in this fucking world and when they hear about those things, and trust me, there are far, far worse things than that one, they should do something instead of simply stating that it's awful, turning away and finishing their greasy fucking cheeseburger."

All I could do was to listen feeling ashamed.

"Recently I told one of my acquaintances the short story of my life," she continued, "his reaction was similar to yours. After a few days he contacted me saying that he wanted to hear more. He moved in to my place for two weeks and we spent every day talking about everything I'd been through. It was hard for him to listen to it, but it was also hard for me to talk about it. Now that man is somewhere in Africa, digging wells in the desert and helping people directly. He's trying to make things better."

"Each and every one of us has a story to tell, or the capacity to hear someone else's story. If we have one, we should tell it, and if we hear one, we should share it with others and pass it on. If we don't, we're simply shutting our eyes to the reality and we leave the world exactly as we found it – crappy."

I admired that kid who had far more life wisdom than me and most of the people I know. Unfortunately, she's become that wise only because she had to experience awful things. And now she was sharing her story with people she may not know that well, hoping to shake them up and wake them up.

Do I have a story? Do I have any life experience that I could share with people and that could, no matter how stupid it may sound, make this world a better place?

No, I do not. How could I, anyway? I was a kid raised in a fairy-tale only starting to live Life in his early twenties.

Still. Maybe I could be a good story sharer? Maybe I could live, collect experiences and share them with others? Was that the one thing I was good at? Will I find peace in this?

There is only one way to find out. I will live, collect stories and experiences and we'll see how it goes.

We spent that night with her friends, having a barbecue in one of the parks after which we left the leftovers in front of a homeless guy's tent. We also went to a disco and I reminded myself once again why I didn't like that kind of place – they are overcrowded, there is too much smoke and the music is way too loud.

We returned home just before the sunrise, falling asleep in the bus on the way back.

"Good night," I said to her as we came in, "thank you for a wonderful evening."

"You're welcome," she replied and went straight to the bathroom not even giving me a hug or a smile and without looking at me.

In a few minutes she entered my room, took all of her clothes off and cuddled next to me.

"Don't worry, I never take advantage of a man on our first date," she whispered and gave me a good night kiss.

Day 294.

I was woken up by the sound of someone turning the doorknob. An older man walked into the room, threw a quick glance at the bed, made eye contact with the stranger who was lying next to his (nude, but covered) niece, took something from the shelf and returned to where he'd come from.

"Someone's just walked into the room," I whispered to Melissa, shaking her softly in order to wake her up, "and I think he's going to kill me when I go out."

"Ooooh, relaaaax," she replied still half asleep, "that's my uncle."

"What do I know about Algerian uncles?" I wasn't very convinced. "I'm not leaving this room if not accompanied by you."

She soon got up, we walked to the kitchen where she introduced me to her flatmates, her uncle and aunt, who greeted me politely, but with caution using basic English.

During breakfast I listened to them talking in some strange language and I could only imagine that their conversation would be much more aggressive if I weren't there. I kept my eyes fixed on the plate until I was done, politely thanked them for their generosity and left the place with Melissa.

"I told him you were my friend and that we'd fallen asleep the last night while we were watching a movie," she told me as we left her building situated in the outskirts of the city.

"Did he believe you?" I asked her.

"I think he did," she said carelessly, "but he lectured me about how it's not a good thing sleeping in the same room with men, especially now when I have my husband coming from Algeria in a few days.

"A husband?" The surprises just kept coming.

"Oh, yes, a husband," she said, a bit sad, "but that's a long story. I'm not in the mood, I have a long and difficult day at the university ahead of me.

We got onto the metro and arranged to meet at the same place during the evening, after she'd done everything she had to do.

She went in the direction of the Sorbonne, and I went in the opposite direction, towards Montmartre.

The day was grey, dull and rainy, not typical of the romantic Paris that I'd expected to find. The narrow streets leading to Montmartre were full of dubious guys who were taking money from passers-by, offering to play a game with three small cups and a marble. They would bugger off the moment they spotted cops.

I observed the interiors of bohemian cafés, expensive restaurants with white table-cloths, bakeries from which wonderful aromas emanated, colourful patisseries, all the while scanning people looking for a cute brunette with bangs who would be standing under her red umbrella with white dots with her eyes fixed drowsily on the clouds or thinking about changing the course of someone's life in a playfully crazy way.

I didn't find her.

I observed street musicians, painters, caricature-makers and entertainers. I saw the signs of tiredness on their faces: you could tell that they'd prefer to stay home on that rainy day instead of selling a part of themselves to tourists.

I browsed souvenir shops and regular shops. I explored the entrances to the buildings where Dalì, Monet, Picasso and Van Gogh had lived. I knew that I was walking down the streets where history took place, streets that even today had an artistic aura, but everything was still grey. And a grey atmosphere always depresses me, no matter where I find myself.

Feeling a bit disappointed I dragged myself to Sacré-Cœur Basilica, one of the most famous monuments in Paris situated in the northern part of the city. I placed myself at the foot of that colossal white building and absorbed what was going on around me. I observed the tourists, the street band that was getting ready to perform a couple of songs, Africans who were trying to sell some bracelets to the tourists. There were all kinds of things. But, still, everything was grey.

And from one moment to another everything changed. The clouds made room for the sun, everything around me became a bit livelier; I could spot in the distance the roofs of Parisian houses in all their glory; the tourist murmur was toned down by an invisible hand, and the band started playing the opening lines of their first song on acoustic guitar – one of my most cherished songs ever – Imagine.

All of a sudden, Paris transformed from a boring sad town into a wonderful and colourful town with bright facades and red roofs, vivacious tourists who, during the sunny afternoon, sit on the stairs of basilica and hum how it would be nice if we *imagined*.

I knew that I'd just experienced the moment by which I would always remember Paris.

I took a stroll along the bank of Seine, visited Notre Dame and returned to the metro station, just in time to meet Melissa.

I didn't find her there, but I did find her uncle. He wasn't there because he was planning to kick my ass or kill me. Instead, he was there to show me the way back home: Melissa had sent him a message saying that she'd be late so he should pick me up.

We walked towards the apartment in silence. We didn't speak the same language but also we felt a bit awkward due to the eye contact we'd shared that morning. We tried not to let the awkwardness of the situation show, but I'm not sure whether we actually succeeded.

As soon as I got into the apartment I ran into my room. An e-mail was waiting for me from Maaike, from Amsterdam:

I've been thinking about you a lot since you've been gone.

It surprises me since I usually don't miss people. But this time I feel that something is different: I feel that you're the person I could learn so many things from, and whose company I would truly enjoy. You're the only person in whose eyes I discern wisdom and who's not fucked up. The fact that you didn't try to take me to bed (and you had a couple of chances) as nearly all men who I meet try to do, made me even more convinced of it.

I know that you're a traveller and that you're on your Journey, but, at the same time, I know that we're not that different. The only thing that is different about the two of us is our situation. You're going somewhere, and I'm not, even though I would want to be headed somewhere, more than anything.

So, what do you say about this idea: come back to Amsterdam, make love to me every day, talk to me about your life over dinner with candles and we'll take long walks on the streets of Amsterdam. Maybe we could even go somewhere together, let's say Spain. I've always wanted to go there. And with you there next to me, it would be amazing.

Say yes. Just like you've been saying to me that accepting everything new and saying 'yes' to the new challenges has changed your life, let the Universe change your life right now. Say yes.

M.

I wasn't sure I wanted to go back to Amsterdam, I wasn't sure I wanted to make love to her and I wasn't sure I wanted to go to Spain with her.

"What should I do?" I asked Melissa as soon as she came home, explaining the whole situation to her.

"What are you afraid of?" she asked me instantly as she did the same thing she'd done the previous night, but this time she kept some pieces of clothing on. She turned on the laptop and started browsing through the photos she'd taken that day. The outfit she was wearing in the photos was identical to the one she was wearing now, the only difference was that in the photos, she wasn't under a cover.

"Most likely, I'm afraid of hurting her," I answered, taking my eyes off the laptop and trying to concentrate on what I was saying and thinking. "I'm not sure that I like her strongly enough to go back to Amsterdam for her and carry on my journey with her. I don't want to give her false hope and promises because I know how much it hurts."

"Everybody knows," she said, "I'm sure she knows it, too, just like I know that she's a big girl who'll know how to handle it. Don't be selfish, please the girl. You see that she wants you. She needs you."

She made a good point. Should I play against myself in these situations and not think about my needs and desires? Should I forget about them all together and become a psychologist, psychiatrist and, above all, friend to the people I run into on my Journey? Should I focus my attention on them and, respecting their wishes, help them to get their lives in order by simply being there? Or at least do my best?

"I agree," I said after brief contemplation. "Still, if I return to Amsterdam I will be losing a lot of time I planned to use for hitchhiking towards the south of the continent. I could get back because that's what she wants, but by when? If I focus my attention on other people and their needs and neglect my needs, in the long run, it will only mean one thing, my ruin. It is impossible to take care of others and not hurt oneself. At least not constantly."

"Work your way around it," she said not taking her eyes off of her laptop. "Find another option. Flights to Spain aren't that expensive. You can suggest to her that she buys you a plane ticket in exchange for your sexual services," she burst out laughing "and then you'll become the person you'd judged just a few days ago, before you'd met me. A prostitute."

I wasn't sure if she was joking or being serious, but I decided to give it good thought.

The fact was that plane tickets from the Netherlands or Belgium to Spain weren't that expensive, only about thirty Euros. However, that thirty Euros, given my budget, equalled almost an entire week longer on the road – a week of adventures, new acquaintances and experiences.

I didn't want to over-think it so I grabbed the laptop from my semi-nude friend and composed an e-mail in which I set forth my sincere doubts:

I could go back to Amsterdam, but there are two problems – first, I'm going to spend a lot of time I was planning to spend on the hitchhiking towards the south and I can't afford a plane ticket; second, even if I had the ticket, I'm not sure whether I could respond to your feelings as you would like me to and I'm not sure whether I would like to continue my journey with you.

I got a reply in less than a couple of minutes.

I bought you a ticket from Brussels to Barcelona. I got myself one, too.
We'll make other arrangements when you get here.
M.

"Wow, colleague," Melissa exclaimed when I read the reply out loud, "I'm so proud of you."

She put away her laptop, pulled me closer and looked me straight in the eye.

"Remember," she whispered "the one who doesn't take risks, never finds out."

Day 299.

As soon as I was back in Amsterdam I ended up in the bed of my new/old host.

With a high temperature and an unbearable stomach-ache.

"Where exactly does it hurt?" she asked me, lying next to me for the second day in a row and rolling the God-knows-what joint in a row.

"Here," I indicated the part under the belly button, grimacing. The night behind me was terrible: I'd spent it curled up in the foetal position paying a visit to the toilet every half hour. To make the whole thing worse, that very same day my health insurance policy, which I'd bought just before I left Zagreb, expired. What if it was appendicitis? Or a hernia? In the middle of the night Lola, the dog, joined me in the bed; I guess she sensed I had some health problems so she cuddled next to me, just next to the part that hurt. Her small body seemed to be emanating benevolent warmth, which helped me a lot to make it through the night.

"Here you go, this will help you," Maaike offered me a spliff and starting rolling herself another one.

"Thank you, but I don't feel like getting high."

"You seem to be forgetting that marijuana is also a medicine," she pointed out.

How could I have forgotten? How many times had I talked in favour of its consumption, mentioning its healing powers and discussing its legalization, giving valid arguments?

I don't smoke cigarettes, I don't drink coffee, I don't drink much alcohol, but I have a habit of smoking a joint every now and then. I'd usually have one after a difficult day. Or not so difficult, it doesn't matter that much. It has a relaxing effect on me, and it has a strange effect on my brain cells: they function completely differently than when I am sober. They seem to be freer, not restrained by the stereotypes that I was taught by society.

Some of the best (but also some of the goofiest) ideas came to me when I was in that state of mind. The following morning, sober, I would reconsider the applicability of those ideas. I discarded most of them instantly, but the rare ones...well, they were precious.

I used it as an entrance to the world of an alternative way of thinking, but also as a sleeping pill and a medicine for loneliness. I'd only heard about its healing powers from articles I'd found online and from other people who talked about its beneficial effects.

However, there I was, in Amsterdam, ready to test its beneficial effects on my own skin.

Still with an intense stomach-ache, I inhaled the first toke. Then the second. I felt the famous sensation spreading through my body and my mind. A few minutes after, I stubbed it out and left the filter in my host's ashtray and tried to leave the bed and take a few steps.

I staggered round to the kitchen and back. The stomach-ache was almost entirely gone. I was cured. And stoned. Two birds...

Since I was no longer distracted by the pain, I could finally start the one thing for which I was in Amsterdam: spend some quality time with Maaike.

She was different that time than the last– probably because of the e-mail she'd sent to me while I was in Paris in which she completely opened up and revealed what was most precious to her – her feelings. She didn't care about shocking me or tickling my imagination with comments or sexual innuendo. She simply talked about her life.

And her life was shocking.

She spent her childhood running away from her parents, being a victim of her father and three stepmothers. She spent her teenage years in violent relationships with older men, she was even raped, and, in her early twenties, encouraged by her then boyfriend, she worked in strip-tease bars as an escort.

She'd left her old life behind her, but you could still see the consequences: the introversion, the lack of trust in people, agoraphobia and demophobia, and in order to overcome all those fears she was smoking five grams of marijuana on a daily basis. That's way too much even for big guys like me.

The reason why Maaike wanted me back in Amsterdam was my lifestyle, which terrified her. Travelling, depending on strangers in unknown places, not knowing where you're going to end up that day or where you're going to sleep. She had to have everything under control, which was basically the last thing I thought about. She wanted some advice, she wanted guidance, and she wanted me to take her with me as some sort of rehabilitation – to cure her. Also, she wanted to listen about my life, which was, compared to hers, tediously beautiful.

It's not that hard to end up with no scars when you're surrounded by your parents' love all the time, when you have two additional mothers – two aunts – who pampered you and your brother, and when your biggest problem is a broken heart.

The conclusion was that, given everything she'd been through, she's turned out quite normal. And now, simply, she didn't have any will to carry on. The only thing she was capable of was living in her apartment, getting social welfare, and leaving the apartment to run some errands and get herself a couple of grams of *Amnesia* and *Afghan Haze*.

While I took some walks down the beloved streets of Amsterdam I thought about the story of her life. I was sure I could help her. I could take her by the hand and take her to another part of Europe and lead her slowly into my lifestyle. I could show her the beauty of freedom, of the unknown and uncertainties.

I could. But I wasn't sure whether I wanted to do it.

I, too, was in the process of rehabilitation from the life I'd been leading as a stockbroker in Zagreb. I wasn't ready to be someone's guide and to show someone how to do something, to be someone's lover. I had a lot of work with myself and I knew that, with her, I would neglect myself.

Moreover, I couldn't respond to her feelings. I wasn't in love with her. I didn't see her as a person that I needed in that moment.

When I returned to Amsterdam, from the very start I'd been honest with her about everything and it was high time that I made the right moves and made some decisions.

"I think I want to go to Spain alone," I said to her three days before we were supposed to get on the plane for Barcelona together. It wasn't easy to say it. I was afraid of hurting her. However, I'd made my decision – honesty was my new policy. Even though I'd always thought of myself as of an honest person, only then did I realize how calculated I'd been in the past. I'd always avoided situations like that one, situations that could lead to a person getting hurt right in front of my eyes. The one thing standing behind it was nothing more than more cowardice, cowardice camouflaged by good intentions.

"Yeah, I knew that you'd make that decision," she said after a short pause, "and I don't have anything to hold against you. You've been honest with me from the very start and I knew that there were some risks involved. And I thank you for it."

And that was that. She got my point; she was being reasonable about it and didn't make a fuss. Honesty really is the best policy. And when you think that I could easily torture myself with a sense of guilt after she bought me, bought us, the plane tickets. I could've stalled, gone around it, tried to inspire her so that she was the one to give up on the journey so that I didn't feel guilty.

However, I did not. And I was proud of it. Still, that was relatively easy. I wasn't sure if I would've done the same thing if I hadn't been dealing with someone I'd only known for a few days. Would I have been that honest, not caring about the consequences? I wasn't sure.

I'd passed the first level of honesty. All I had to do was keep on going with it.

"Rose invited me to visit her in Prague, and I think that I'll do it!" – that was the text message I received as I was on my way to the airport in Brussels.

It was a wonderful text message. Rose was a girl from Amsterdam whom I'd met during my first visit to the city and whom I'd introduced to Maaike a couple of days before. In less than five minutes they found a mutual language, became friends and now Rose was inviting her to go with her to the city she's moving to in a few days.

The universe took the cards in its hands, shuffled them and arranged the rest of the game. Maaike was going to Prague as part of her therapy and I was going on my new adventure, alone. In the end, everybody won.

With a smile on my face I put my sleeping bag on the floor at the airport intending to doze off a bit before I fly to Barcelona.

Day 305.

I started noticing that the Spanish didn't speak much English soon after I got off the plane, and my suspicion were confirmed when I started hitchhiking from the airport to the city. A cab driver pulled over.

He mumbled something in Spanish, and I replied in the same way, only in English. He looked confused.

"No *dinero*," I said with a smile on my face slowly walking away from the car.

"Mmhmm, mmhmm, *peaje*," he replied using one of the few Spanish words whose meaning I knew. *Peaje*. I'd heard it in France when I was hitchhiking, the only difference was that the French version was *péage*. Even though it wasn't exactly the same I guessed the meaning was the same: toll booths.

I made a logical conclusion: the good taxi driver would give me a ride from the airport in Girona to the toll booths, which weren't that far away. It would be easier for me to hitchhike to Barcelona, almost one hundred kilometres away.

I thanked him sincerely and got into the taxi.

In less than a couple of minutes we arrived to the toll booths, but we didn't stop there. As there was a dead silence in the car I didn't dare to mention anything. I assumed that he wanted to drop me off at a better place for hitchhiking. However, I didn't get an opportunity to confirm my assumption.

I kept quiet and enjoyed my first impressions of the new country I was in. The driver, too, kept quiet and kept on driving.

Only when we came close to Barcelona did it occurred to me that the taxi driver maybe wanted me to *pay* the toll as he would give me a ride all the way to the city. After all, it was possible that in Spanish, the words 'toll' and 'toll booths' were exactly the same.

I got the confirmation some hundred metres ahead when we arrived to the toll booths.

"Mmhmm, mmhmm, *dinero*," the driver said, indicating with his thumb and index finger the well-known sign for money.

"No *dinero*," I repeated the same sentence that I used when I was getting into the taxi. I also made a face that I hoped was showing how sorry I was for the misunderstanding.

He wasn't quite satisfied with my answer, let alone the expression on my face. He was persistent in getting his six Euros for the toll.

Since I'm not a person prone to conflict, I got the bag where I kept my money and shook out all the coins I had. I had about three Euros in coins. I offered them to him.

When he saw me shaking out those coins, a heap of yellow coins, and the look in my eyes he mumbled something, turned around and kept on driving. He didn't stop until we got to a certain point where I got out and started searching for my new CS hosts.

It was the eleventh town I found myself in during my journey and each of those towns I had a host through the CouchSurfing site. All those months of hosting people in Zagreb truly paid off.

My hosts lived in the suburbs of Barcelona, in a large villa with a pool and a tennis court. They would normally rent their villa to tourists, but when there weren't too many tourists, out of the peak tourist season, they would host CouchSurfers. The CouchSurfers, to repay them, would help around the house, wash the dirty clothes and help themselves to the remains in the fridge – nearly for free.

Fair exchange.

Since my hosts were pretty occupied, they didn't have time for the most important thing when you come to visit someone – taking them to see the city, taking them to have a drink with their friends, in other words, making them feel like a local, and not just another tourist who had come to visit the famous Spanish city.

I wandered around Barcelona, just like in Paris not long before I listened to the street musicians, took a walk to the sea, admired the crane above Sagrada Familia and the entrance fee to the House of God. I took a walk around the markets in the open, Gaudí's park, laid around the tourist beach with a bottle of beer.

I liked the city, but I didn't like being there on my own.

When I returned to the villa, just like many times before, I threw a glance at the map of Europe and chose my next destination – Valencia.

I had only a month left before I returned home because that was when my exam session started and I was sure that I would find a cheap flight from Spain or Portugal to central Europe. After all, Maaike had paid 24 Euros for the plane ticket from Brussels to Barcelona, luggage and taxes included.

While I was making a plan to return home I received a reply from my potential host in Valencia. It was negative. It was only the second negative reply I got since I started my adventure, the first one being the one from Copenhagen and that one took me to Amsterdam, which was the reason why I was where I was. Still, I didn't feel like changing my route this time. I sent another request to the same city and went for a drink with the hosts and their guests.

The following morning there was a reply waiting for me:

I've just returned from my hitchhiking adventure in Scandinavia, so how could I say 'no' to a fellow hitchhiker? I don't have a couch in my apartment, but I've got space on the floor and, somehow I'm sure you're not looking for comfort. Try to be here as soon as possible because tomorrow I'm going with my friends on a trip to the mountains nearby where we will do some rock climbing, so it would be great if you could come with us.

See you soon in Montpellier, B.

Wait a minute. Montpellier? It's in the south of France. And I'd sent an e-mail to Valencia the previous night.

I dug through my e-mails and remembered everything. The previous night, after having a few drinks with the hosts, I came to my room and saw that I got another negative reply from Valencia. Feeling quite disappointed and hurt since two people from the same city obviously didn't want me as their guest, I impulsively threw a glance at the map and chose the complete opposite direction – the south of France. I sent a drunk e-mail to the first person in the first city I came across and that was it.

Now I had a place to stay in Montpellier. And not only that, I was invited to go rock climbing, that is if I managed to get there by the following day, after all, it was only three hundred kilometres away. I knew it would be difficult because it would take me at least five or six hours to get there.

Unless I went straight away. In that way I would definitely arrive there in time. It's not like I had any other plan or reservation. I packed my backpack, said goodbye to my hosts, caught the train to leave the city and found a perfect place to start hitchhiking, a gas station on the road going eastward.

Oh, the freedom of making decisions.

The very same evening, after five hours on the road and with three rides behind me, I was drinking wine with my new French friends.

Day 309.

"Being a man is a huge advantage," Caroline said to me as we were walking to the nearby mountain where we were supposed to go rock climbing. She had thick curly red-brown hair, a face covered with freckles and gorgeous brown eyes. I'd met her at the welcome party where we'd exchanged a couple of glances. As opposed to the previous evening, she wasn't wearing any makeup now, which made her at least twice as beautiful.

"I would never dare to travel on my own, being a girl and all that."

"I wouldn't either, if I was cute as you," I tried to be funny, seductive and not sleazy, all at the same time, "but you're only alone while you're waiting for someone to give you a ride. Once somebody picks you up, you're in the company of the driver, and once you arrive to your destination you're with your hosts and their friends. Just like you're keeping me company now."

"Have you ever had any awkward experiences?" she wanted to know.

"Not a single one," I answered readily, "but hey, who knows, I'm only starting."

"And you're not afraid?" she was curious.

"Not really," I said self-assuredly, "before I met people who travelled like this I also thought that it's impossible not to be afraid, that you have to be the bravest person in the world. But each and every person whom I hosted kept on explaining to me that I needed courage just to get myself going. Later all the pieces fall into place. And I really have to say that it's totally true. Also, I believe that the fact that I'm completely reckless, that I didn't think about the negative situations I could find myself in, helped quite a bit. Negative thoughts normally don't lead you anywhere, they only discourage you."

She kept on listening, and I kept on talking. I told her about the most interesting situations from my trips, leaving out only one. I enjoyed it, and she seemed to be enjoying it, too.

While I was hosting people in my apartment, for most of the time, I was the one listening carefully, absorbing all the stories and fantasizing about embarking on a similar adventure one day myself. And look at me now: I was the one travelling around, staying at other people's places and sharing incredible stories with an interested audience who saw me in the same light as I'd seen those who would spend a couple of days on my shabby blue sofa. Stimulation. Encouragement. Inspiration. And, in return, I got so many things: their time, their attention and their company. I made friendships wherever I went, as if I'd always belonged there.

The same thing happened during that afternoon we spent together rock climbing, laughing, having fun. I spent most of the time with Caroline, both because the instant closeness we felt and because her English was the best.

However, she was the worst with the climbing rope. She nearly killed me on one occasion since she hadn't fastened my rope tight enough. I was only left with a small cut on my right shin that will remain there for the rest of my life.

"Thank you for that." I was mocking her on our way back showing her the cut she caused. "Scars are my favourite souvenirs, they don't cost me anything and they save me the space in my backpack."

"I'm really sorry," she said humbly, "you can come over to my place for dinner so I can make it up to you. If you want to, you can also spend the night on my couch."

It took me only a second to imagine how that evening could turn out. And it was a very tempting image.

"Thanks for the invitation, but I will have to turn it down," I replied gently not wanting to start something that would be over soon. "Tomorrow morning I have to head off early and get on the road."

"Well, good luck then," she said giving me a firm, warm and long hug.

"If you ever find yourself in Zagreb, give me a call," I said, giving her a kiss on her left cheek, "if I'm home, I'd be pleased if you made me dinner."

"Be careful what you wish for, it may come true." She smiled at me in a French way, giving me a kiss on my right cheek.

Day 318.

The longest part of the journey was ahead of me. 830 kilometres from Draguignan to Zürich. The route through Italy was, indeed, a bit shorter by about one hundred kilometres, but I'd decided to avoid the country known for drivers who don't show much understanding of poor hitchhikers.

Still, I had a wonderful tour around the south of France behind me. After Montpellier I'd visited Marseille, Aix-en-Provence and Nice, after which I'd spent a few days camping in the middle of a forest near Draguignan.

Apart from wonderful people and cute places, that period was marked by a thought: I was ready to go back home.

So many things had happened in the previous couple of weeks since I left Zagreb. I needed some time to work it all out in my head, to analyze and to realize what I could learn from everything. Several times I caught myself thinking more about everything that had happened than about the adventures that lay ahead of me. And that was always a good sign to take a break. Take a break from everything, not only from travelling.

I was low in energy, not only because I had so many kilometres behind me, but also because the bunch of new people I'd met and the amount of stories I'd shared with them, and also because of those talks I'd had with the drivers who had given me a ride. Add to that the fact that I'd lost over twenty pounds. When you're on the road all the time and when you're on a budget, the pounds seem to melt away.

I planned my route for the following ten days, across Switzerland, Austria, and then to Slovenia where I had a couple of friends whom I'd hosted in Zagreb. I decided to pay them a visit. I would be back home just in time to start studying for my final exams.

I started hitchhiking early in the morning and got on really well with good drivers, so I was hoping I'd manage to arrive in Zürich the same day. However, all hope was gone when I lost two hours for the simple reason that I forgot to tell one driver where I would be getting out.

So, I arrived to French-Swiss border during the evening with a lot of kilometres ahead of me. And the night was one of the greatest enemies of every hitchhiker. My messy appearance didn't help me a lot thanks to my stupid decision that I wouldn't be shaving until I got back home. Also, the weather condition wasn't very good – it was freezing cold.

During November, Switzerland is very cold. I learned that while I was walking to the border along the highway when I had to put on the warmest clothes I had. I crossed the border without any problem, but the policeman who was on duty showed me the way to a by-road explaining to me that I couldn't hitchhike at the actual border, even though that was the place where everyone would slow down, which was exactly what I needed to resurrect my hope of making it to my destination in time. That way, my chances were slim to none.

Unexpectedly, the Swiss drivers showed mercy to the bearded hitchhiker and a couple of them gave me rides of a few kilometres. I was finally on the road back to Zürich. Still, it was 9 pm and I was in Nyon with more than two hundred kilometres of road with not so much traffic on it ahead of me.

Soon I had to make a decision: would I spend the night somewhere along the road in my summer sleeping bag, with the temperature approaching zero, or would I go to the highway, on foot, and try to walk to the first gas station. There I would actually have a chance of finding a car going in my direction, or of finding a restaurant where I could spend the night. However, in that case, I would be taking the risk of having a close encounter with the Swiss police.

Backpack on my back, headphones in my ears and straight to the highway.

I was walking fast along the road, on the grass, hoping to be invisible to the drivers. I wasn't that surprised when, after only a hundred metres, I heard a police siren behind me.

"Get in!" he ordered in English with a strong French accent.

I did so without hesitating, trying to see the bright side – I wasn't cold anymore and we would be going in the direction I had to go if I wanted to arrive in Zürich. Maybe, just as at the beginning of my journey in Austria, they would leave me at the first gas station and forgive me for breaking the law.

"Are you insane?" the policeman sitting on the driver seat asked looking at me, "walking like that along the highway with headphones in your ears. Do you have any idea about how dangerous it is?"

"I know," I replied amiably, "but I had no choice. I was hitchhiking and a man left me here so I was forced to keep on walking looking for a refuge."

"I don't care," he said sharply and shut up. He started the car and started driving eastward.

"We'll have to write you a ticket for disruption of traffic," the other policeman said after a while. "Do you have any money?"

I reached in my pocket and took out one Euro and twenty cents.

"It's all I've got."

"Well, are you some kind of a thief?" he started shouting. "Where do you sleep, what do you eat?"

"You know, there's this web page called CouchSurfing..."

"I don't care," he interrupted, obviously very frustrated. "Do you have any money on your credit card?"

"I have a debit card, but I'm not sure whether it works in Switzerland," I replied quietly.

Everyone in the car kept quiet for the rest of the ride.

I've never been in an official police car before, at least not on duty. They forgot all about me and did their job. They were checking the speed of the other drivers, turning a light on vehicles, checking for any suspicious activities; they made a few radio calls in which they explained something to central, or whatever.

We passed a gas station. I was hoping that they would kick me out of the car warning me not to do it ever again, but they simply passed it without changing direction.

After tens of kilometres the highway was closed. All traffic was diverted through a small village and there were, even in the middle of the night, tons of cars trailing in a long line. My drivers drove me to an ATM and told me to try and withdraw twenty francs to pay the ticket.

I thought of two things: I could do what they wanted me to do and try to hitchhike from there while all those cars were still there, or I could take a risk and pretend that my card doesn't work, risking ending up in a police station. That wouldn't be so bad: I would have a place to spend the night, maybe even a warm meal, but while I was walking to the ATM I remembered that I had a souvenir from Amsterdam in my backpack – ten seeds of certain plant and if they caught me with it I don't think they would accept my explanation that it was my cure for stomach-ache.

I withdrew money, took the piece of paper with my ticket, listened to their well-intended advice to go to a nearby train station, happily headed off to the road and, with a smile on my face, stuck out my thumb.

The cars were passing by and so were the minutes. Finally, there were only a couple of cars left. If only I had shaved.

It was 1 a.m. A feeling of total helplessness crept over me. The cold remained my faithful companion. The smile directed at the drivers who were passing became more and more artificial.

At that very same moment, as usually happens at the moment of greatest need, a few meters away from me a car pulled over. Its licence plates said Bern. Okay, it wasn't Zürich, but it was half way there. I ran to the car while the driver opened the passenger door.

"Sprechen Sie Deutch?" my saviour asked me.

"Nein," I replied wondering what I had been doing in high school during my German lessons, which I had three times a week, "English?"

"Yes, okay," he said "where are you from?"

"From Croatia."

"From Croatia?" he asked, in my mother tongue, "I studied in Zagreb back in the seventies."

What were the odds?

So we talked a bit in a language which, despite all the years that had passed, he still hadn't forgotten. He told me that he had studied Slavic languages. He could still easily remember the student protests of '71. Well, my good man, I thought to myself, the students weren't like that anymore. They wouldn't fight for their own rights, let alone those of their colleagues, or because of the situation in the country. Luc was a French man working in Switzerland as a cultural attaché at the French embassy.

As we were approaching Bern, driving down an almost empty road, I started thinking about what I should do next. I only had some one hundred kilometres to my destination, but even if I made it to Zürich, my host Tom, cool guy I hosted in Zagreb, would probably be sleeping. It was two a.m.

As if my driver was reading my mind, he asked me where I was planning to sleep.

"Most probably somewhere by the road; I have a sleeping bag so I'll wait till the morning and carry on," I said, hoping that...

"No way," he interrupted me, making my unspoken wish come true, "you'll be my guest tonight."

And so, after twenty hours on the road, I ended up in the apartment of the French cultural attaché working in Switzerland. He gave me a room, a comfortable bed and a towel, apologizing for having to wake me up early the following morning because he would have to go to work.

"Luc, my friend, don't apologize," I said looking at him as if he was my best friend, "I can't thank you enough for everything you've done for me."

The following morning he woke me up, prepared me breakfast, gave me his business card and, in addition, gave me a ride to the city suburbs. As a salute he wished me luck, but I knew I wouldn't need it, as long there were people like him in this world.

Day 331.

"What's that shit on your face?" Those were Filip's first words when he picked me up in the centre of Zagreb, after which we sat in the car and he dropped me off at my parents' house. It'd been exactly sixty days since we'd seen each other. I'd travelled nine countries with a budget of three hundred Euros, couchsurfed in every city I'd been to, hitchhiked for more than six thousand kilometres, but the first thing I had to explain was why my face was covered by a two-month beard.

I knew straight away that I was home, in a different world with a different set of rules.

The following months were extremely difficult. I fell into the routine of life in Zagreb, even worse than before I started travelling. After having lived on my own for three years I was back at my parents' place, so I couldn't host CSers and I was forced to study to pass the last exams I had left.

Nothing made sense to me. After my intense experiences around Europe, Zagreb was somehow small and boring, while the studying for my boring exams nearly drove me crazy. I was trying to find a chance to escape, but there didn't seem to be one.

I was trapped, I kept thinking about my last adventure, which I perceived as an indicator of how a life should be every day: high intensity, different events, new acquaintances, different places.

Months were passing by. Nothing extraordinary happened except that I passed a few exams and I was getting closer to finishing an important chapter in my life: I was only one exam away from getting my degree, the marketing exam. My head was still swarming with the ideas of running away abroad and finding a job to repay my debt.

The problem was that I had a Croatian passport, which didn't facilitate the process of finding a job in any country; on the contrary, it only made it more difficult. I could go to Australia, to the USA or to Scandinavia as a tourist and work illegally there.

"Come and live with me in Paris, I'll find you a job," Melissa sent me a message one day; she was also in debt for God-knows-what reasons, but she was paying them off slowly. God knew how.

"I have a few friends who could get you inside, you'd have everything you need and you could make even more money than me."

Jammed up by the depression and lack of ideas about what to do next and how to repay my huge debt, I gave that option a serious thought. I really thought about going to Paris, living with her and doing the same job she was doing – being a gigolo.

For many nights, before I fell asleep, I considered the moral aspect of the whole story. How would I feel later? How would I treat old and wrinkled clients? Does the end really justify the means even in situations like that one?

Or maybe I should simply rob a bank? That would be much easier to accept because I didn't see an alternative way.

Day 794.

"What is your daily budget when you travel?" Daniela asked me.
"Less than ten dollars a day."
"What can you afford with the budget like that?"
"Well, everything I need. I get around by hitchhiking, I stay at other CouchSurfers', I buy food in supermarkets, I cook with my hosts..."

I wanted to say to her that it wasn't always easy. From the perspective of other people, it must appear quite an adventure, the biggest adventure in the world, constant excitement, happiness, joy.

However, the truth was that you had to survive all those moments of loneliness, cold and hunger. You can find yourself in different challenging situations when you start wondering whether your actions were right and when you want to change your current situation for a warmer, cosier one...one where there are more people and your stomach is fuller. Travellers aren't vaccinated against melancholy, sadness or nostalgia.

In moments like those, the positive factor was, no matter how strange it may sound, the lack of choice. Friends, the warmth of a home, food: everything is far away. It is unreachable. So there is nothing you can do, you have to pull yourself together and survive. Once you survive, you add a few points of pride, adaptability, experience to your life's account, which might come in handy.

"Were you ever broke?"
"Yes, it happens every now and then. In the south of Spain, on my second longest journey, I ended up in a hippy village north of Gibraltar..."

Day 528.

"Listen, son, I haven't got anything else to say to you, just take care of yourself," my Mom told me as she was walking me to the main train station from where I would get the train for Venice, "and don't forget to call us every day."

"Don't worry, Mom," I gave her a strong hug, "trust me, one day all of this will make much more sense."

The love of my parents was immense and I knew it. Still, they didn't understand me. It wasn't a new thing, they haven't been able to understand me since a couple of years before when I was beginning my third year at university, and I'd told them that I was moving out.

"If you leave, don't come back ever again," that was one of my Dad's threats when I announced my intentions. Mom, as usual, kept on staring sadly at the floor.

"You have your own room, you can get to the centre in twenty minutes if you go by train, the car is always at your disposal, but you always want more," my father said.

"What do you want from me? You left home right after you finished high school." I was fighting back. "And you moved to Zagreb, five hundred kilometres from home and your folks."

"You little bastard, I left my home 'cause I had to," he carried on quite upset, "every month I had to send money to my mother so she could feed my five brothers and sisters. Your mother and I've been working our asses off for our whole lives, we've never been to a nice restaurant or gone out to have a drink with our friends so we could afford stuff for school and clothes for your brother and you. And this is how you repay us."

He was right, but stubborn, persistent and proud as I was, I didn't care. Just like I didn't care about when they warned me to be careful with the stock market business and the money people were lending me. I was convinced that I knew best.

And I always wanted to prove it.

Finally I did move out, but I was so cunning that they didn't even realize it for a whole year. I rented an apartment with a roommate, we split the rent and the bills. I told him that he was free to live there and all I wanted was free access to the place whenever I wanted to.

Every other night I would make up a different excuse for my not sleeping at home. I had to stay at the university late, I had to study with my friends, I missed the train…anything just so I could stay at our rented apartment and do whatever I wanted to do as often as possible.

After a year, or maybe even sooner, they saw right through me, after which they talked to me in a civilised way and then I moved out for real. I lived with my roommate for two years, and my parents paid me a visit only once. They stayed for ten minutes.

"If only we knew who made you like that," was their favourite phrase back in those days.

"If only we knew who made you like that," – that is their favourite phrase even today, when I was leaving for the opposite end of the continent.

I knew that my actions hurt them. I knew that they'd invested their whole life in making the lives of my brother and I better than theirs was. I knew that they were always there for me and that always, really always, I could count on my parents' love. I knew they'd even had too much patience with me and that they'd been putting up with my stubbornness since I was a kid. I knew that they couldn't understand my lifestyle, which was completely different from what they were used to, and that they were in constant fear for me whenever I was travelling, hitchhiking, sleeping at strangers' houses and apartments.

However, all things taken into consideration I knew that I couldn't give up on my Journey because it was, after all, MY journey. I knew that I'd always learnt from my own mistakes, that others were often right when they warned me of something, but I also knew that I'd never regretted any of those lessons. I cherished those moments the same as any other moment because I knew that they made me complete. And I was always ready to go against everyone, not knowing what was waiting for me and not caring about it.

There is only one way to find out what is waiting for you around the corner: go and take a look.

I felt sorry for my parents. If I'd been able to, I would've chosen someone else for them as a son, someone who would listen to them since the son they had only created problems, no matter how hard he wanted to make them proud.

"Do you like Venice?" Sarah asked me few moments after we met.

Sarah was a girl whom I'd come across on the CouchSurfing site, but as I didn't plan to spend the night in Venice I only took her to have a drink and take a stroll down the streets of the most romantic city in the world, where she lived and studied. My flight from Milan to Seville was scheduled for the following day. It was sponsored by my brother Filip who, by buying me the plane ticket, managed to prevent me from hitchhiking across half of Europe in order to arrive to Spain.

"Well, frankly, not really," I was being honest, "I've already been here twice and it's always over-crowded with tourists. And it stinks."

That made her laugh. She changed the subject and showed me around the city. We talked, we laughed, we hung out as if we'd known each other for years, instead of only an hour. I was genuinely happy: there was a new adventure in front of me and the tedious everyday life of Zagreb was behind me. Talking to Sarah I realized that I was full of energy, that everything was more colourful, that I started noticing all those details which I'd been neglecting and that a smile never left my face.

We passed next to the busy Rialto bridge, and soon we were in narrow streets without a single tourist. I instantly felt as if I were in another city, much more beautiful, calmer and more relaxed. I no longer felt that I was in a city with a million tourists, but in a city where people actually live, work, go to school, fall in love, have a beer on a park bench. Venice was glowing.

And the main reason for its glow was walking right next to me.

I remembered Sofia and my conclusion that every city was as beautiful as the people who live there, the people you meet and with whom you spend some time. Venice was wonderful now.

Sarah took me to a place where they made her favourite sandwiches, showed me the side of Venice you usually don't have the opportunity to see. We laid back on a wooden pier and observed the immense blue surface above us, trying to interpret the meaning of the forms the clouds took. Finally, we ended up in a park.

"I had no idea that there were parks in Venice," I exclaimed ecstatically, "this city really starts to get under my skin."

She smiled bashfully, gave me a kiss on a cheek and informed me that she had to leave me for an hour because she had some lessons at the university.

I sat on the soft green grass, right next to a patch of clover.

"Wouldn't it be awesome if I found a four-leaf..." I thought and spotted one instantly. I picked it up and saved it so I could give it to Sarah.

I made myself cosy on the grass and, with a giant smile on my face, realized that life was full of small signs, if people only cared to notice them. And look for them. I took out a new small notebook to write down some of my thoughts about the day when I noticed a sticker on the cover of the notebook, a sticker I had almost completely forgotten about. Nina had given it to me as a going-away present. There was an illustrated sheep on the sticker and – a four-leaf clover.

I laughed, reached into my backpack and took out a small stuffed sheep. Another gift from Nina.

"I know it's not your birthday, but I had to buy it for you," she said to me as she was handing me the stuffed sheep "it reminded me of you."

"Really?" I looked at the small stuffed creature, which had a satisfied look on its face and half-open eyes as if it'd been smoking something of good quality. "In what way?"

"By the horoscope, by the expression of its face and by its lifestyle," she replied.

"Its lifestyle?" I understood the first two associations.

"Well, yes," she continued self-assuredly, "it's a sheep, but it's not limited by its herd. She went away from her shepherd and the sheepdog and now, with a smile on her face, she's travelling the world and doing what she pleases. Just like you."

"Shouldn't I be a black sheep then?" I liked the story very much.

"No way," she was sharp, "black sheep try so hard to be different from everyone else that they end up being completely absorbed and burdened by it. Being different and having an alternative lifestyle becomes their ultimate goal, they stop thinking about what is right for them and what isn't. You're not like that. Sometimes you act like the majority, sometimes like the minority. That's why the sheep is white. You are no different to others by your appearance, but you are by what is inside you. And that could serve you one day, as camouflage."

"I see," I gave her a grateful look. "Thank you."

"You're welcome," she responded in the same way. "Take care of it. It will take care of you, too."

I had my stuffed sheep and the four-leaf clover I'd just found. And I was writing in a notebook with a sticker with a sheep and a four-leaf clover on it. I didn't try to find a deeper meaning in it all, it just seemed to me as a very good sign for the first day of my new trip.

Day 546.

It had been two weeks and I wasn't very satisfied with what I'd been through. I'd been to Seville, Huelva, Punta Umbria and Quarteira, a small town in the south of Portugal. I'd contacted a couple of CouchSurfers, met them, met their friends, the friends of their friends, stayed at different places. We spent the days on the sandy beaches, under the palm trees, with *tapas* and *cervezas* and Moroccan chocolate. Time went by, it was fun and eventful, but, somehow, I was missing something.

It bothered me. I hadn't come to the Iberian peninsular to party and have fun. I could do the same thing at the Croatian seaside. I'd come there to experience something new, learn Spanish, find interesting stories, test myself in unpredictable situations. But I wasn't doing any of those things.

That was the reason why, after getting up one morning in a Portuguese village, I decided to change tactics.

All I knew was the direction – east. I had a couple of people in mind that I wanted to visit, but apart from that I didn't have anything else planned. I decided to get myself to the Road and let it take me where it thought was best for me. Whatever happened would be fine.

"There, already on your first day I'll give you a new experience," she informed me during the very same day, just as I was cursing it and my decision. I'd been standing under the scorching June sun for five hours and I hadn't moved more than fifty kilometres. I was hungry and thirsty and far away from any place where I could satisfy my basic physical needs.

"What, are you talking about dehydration, starvation or something else?" I was mocking it.

"Pussy," she responded, in the same manner, "negativity will never bring you anywhere and you know that. A positive attitude, your thumb firmly stuck out and a smile on your face. Let me see you."

I listened involuntarily. However, I was in her realm, on the hot asphalt, so I had to show some sort of respect. The same thing I did when I came to someone's home.

"You see…" she whispered ten minutes later when the first car pulled over.

The driver was a middle-aged man with a joint in his mouth. He didn't understand one word of English, but, feeling rather encouraged by a sudden rush of optimism, I perceived that fact as a good thing: I would get free private lessons in Spanish. Or at least, I could practise the universal language, body language.

And I was doing it really well. For starters, I took a puff he offered me.

Helping myself with the basic Spanish I'd learnt from audio lessons I carried with me, I tried to explain to him who I was and what I was doing there. It seemed it was working: he was thrilled so he decided to take me to have a beer and meet some of his friends.

Even though it meant that I would be losing a couple of hours of precious time, I'd given a promise to the Road and now I had to play the game.

He drove me around the tourist destinations, sunny beaches, etc., rolled another joint and took me to his *amigos* for a *cerveza*. He told everyone my story, and the drinks kept coming one after another. There were some very delicious snails involved. I simply let myself go.

"I'm not that impressed." I sent a thought to miss Road. "It's been a nice experience, but it's not really a new one. I've been in similar wonderful situations like this one before."

"This wasn't my intention," she replied calmly, "you have to be patient."

I patiently had another beer and got back to the car so my new friend could give me a ride to the border with Spain.

"Wanna Coke?" I thought he asked.

"No, thank you," I replied.

A few moments after that, he stopped the car in a parking lot, took out his wallet and some white powder which he had in a fold of aluminium foil. He made a line on a credit card using another credit card.

Ah, that coke.

"You're good," I told the Road after I got out of the car right next to the non-existent border. I was waiting for the next car with my eyes wide open. "But this isn't my first experience like this either. Do you remember who you sent me the first time I hitchhiked?"

"That wasn't my intention either" she replied. "You have to be patient."

"Whatever you say." I was calm. "Still, could you, please, hurry up? It's getting dark."

"He he he" I thought I could hear her, somewhere in the distance.

I managed to stop a couple of cars, but they could only give me a ride for a few kilometres, and I didn't experience anything new. I was fooled.

It was getting dark, I was many kilometres away from a town where I knew people whom I could call and arrange to spend the night on their couch. Perhaps one of the drivers who'd picked me up would show mercy on me and ask me to spend the night at their place, or...

"Aha!" I got it. "Is this what you have in store for me today? Sleeping under the stars? Well, thanks a lot."

"You're being a pussy again." She was disappointed. "I've done everything I could to bring you people who could only give you a short ride so you could have a new experience, just like I promised, and all you do is whine."

"But, what if I get torn up by wolves?" I wasn't giving up so easily.

"There you go with your negative attitude again." She, on the other hand, seemed to be giving up. "Look on the bright side." She accentuated the word 'bright'. I didn't know why, but I decided to stop with the whining. After all, she was right, it'd never taken me anywhere.

Since I had only an hour left until the night came, I gave up hitchhiking and started searching for a safe place to spend the night. Luckily, I had a tent with me, which a girl whom I'd met when I came to Spain had given me. It wasn't all that bad.

However, I wasn't feeling at ease. No matter how brave (or reckless?) I was when hitchhiking and couchsurfing around Europe I was still a bit afraid of spending the night at the side of the road. That one night in the bushes of Croatia seemed so far away. Would anyone see me, attack me, rob me? True, I was beside the road, far away from inhabited areas, much taller than anyone else and I didn't carry anything valuable with me. Whoever decided to mess with me wouldn't be that lucky.

In fact, the thing that scared me most were wild animals, which might come across me.

I found an area where the grass was high so it could protect me from being spotted; it was an ideal position to set up the tent since it was surrounded by the road on three sides. That was supposed to keep away the wild animals, if there were any.

I set up the tent, had dinner, which included a banana and some cookies I'd bought in the last place I'd made a stop in. I played on my mp3 player an Australian band that brought memories, lit a joint and observed a magnificent sunset.

However, the magnificence was only starting. As the sun set, the stars started showing up, one by one. After an hour they covered the entire sky.

Freedom suddenly had a new dimension.

"Thank you," I said, grateful for the experience the Road had prepared

for me. "I can't wait to see what you have in store for me for the rest of
this journey."

"Just let yourself go," she replied, "have faith."

Day 558.

After a starry night near Seville I spent a couple of days on a farm in Facinas, slept on a beach in Cádiz, attended a CS meeting at the southern-most point of continental Europe, cape Tarifa, met my friends from Sofia in La Linea and hung out with monkeys in Gibraltar.

"If you head north you'll come across quite an interesting place" the first driver who picked me up in Gibraltar told me, "a little village at the top of a hill, with an old castle in the centre, where the hippies live. I think you'd like it."

I didn't pay attention to him or to his advice. I was convinced that I wanted to arrive at my destination that same day, a little town some one hundred kilometres eastward, where I would be helping a lady around the house in exchange for food and accommodation. I'd even set myself a challenge: while I am at her place, I wouldn't be withdrawing any money from an ATM, I would try to get by with the ten Euros I had with me.

"Dammit!" I yelled as loud as I could, only a minute after I got out of the car. I'd left the road map of Spain, my only method of orientation, in the car.

"Why are you doing this to me?" I asked the Road angrily.

She kept quiet. Perhaps she was also angry with me for some reason. Or maybe she just didn't want to give me answers; perhaps she wanted me to think about it a bit and to ask myself where the bad karma came from.

"Have faith," was the last sentence I had heard from her, a couple of weeks before when I decided to give myself up to her, back when I'd promised that I wouldn't follow my plans blindly but would let her show me the way.

Did I have faith? Was I sticking to our agreement on spontaneity? Were my eyes wide open searching for signs that could appear anywhere around me?

"Where to?" A lady in a white car asked me using perfect English, pulling over even though I was sitting by the curb and thinking.

"I don't know," I said.

"You don't know?" She was surprised. "Then, what are you doing by the road if you don't know where you're going?"

"I'm thinking," I shrugged, "and where are you going?"

"Casteller de la Frontera," she pronounced a name of an unknown town, "it's twenty kilometres from here on a small hill..."

"...and there is a castle where hippies live," I finished her sentence, feeling my heartbeat speeding up.

"Yes, how did you know?" she was confused.

"Oh" I sighed, realizing why I'd lost the map, "can I go with you?"

"Sure," she opened the passenger door.

As we were driving up the hill to our destination in a car that sounded like it was dying on us, she told me a few details about the place in which she lived. In that way I found out that the castle was built by the Moors during their conquer of Spain, after which they had left similar buildings and monuments.

During the seventies, the town was completely abandoned and the inhabitants were moved to a village nearby, Nuevo Castellar, which was more modern. At the same time, attracted by the beauty of the village, wonderful climate, loose laws and the proximity of Morocco, the village was inhabited by hippies, mostly from Germany. They moved in the abandoned houses and, protected by the law, transformed the village into a hippy oasis. Today, only a few traces of that period were left and only a couple of flower children, just as the castle was the only remaining building in a village that stood as a testimony of another era.

"Take care," the lady warned me, leaving me on a street in the village, "we're far from hippy ideals, so be careful about who you trust. Not everyone is well-intentioned."

I thanked her for her advice and the ride, and started exploring the place.

It was a village like every other. I passed by a café, a market, a children's playground, a hotel next to the castle. There were no indications that would tell me that I was in a hippy village. The people weren't different from others in Andalusia, nobody wore colourful dresses, had joints in their mouths or flowers in their hair.

Behind a garden fence I spotted an old man who didn't appear as if he were from there: he was tall, pale with long grey hair and a messy beard. I approached him, greeted him politely and asked him whether he needed help with something saying that I was ready to do anything in exchange for food and a place to sleep.

He looked at me with contempt, not stopping what he was doing; he lowered his eyes denying me an answer.

Feeling a bit disappointed and filled with doubt about my spontaneous decision to come there, I sat on the street and started making bracelets. I learnt that skill a couple of months before and I put it into practice whenever I had some time to kill. I would sometimes make souvenirs for the friends I met travelling or as a gift for my hosts. Maybe I could start selling them and, in that way, try to make some money to buy something to eat.

It was early afternoon and still too early to start looking for a place to set up my tent.

"Hey!" a stranger called me while walking slowly towards me. He was old, or at least he appeared old, skinny, wrinkled, with small eyes, pronounced cheekbones and a hoarse voice. He had shoulder-length messy hair, a moustache and transparent blue eyes. He was with a blind girl, who was lame and had a disfigured face, probably a consequence of a car accident.

"Hey!" I responded in the same way, trying to fight back the sense of discomfort that thrilled through my body.

"Where are you from?" he asked me automatically, not showing a particular interest, while the girl was standing still next to him with her eyes hidden under dark shades.

"From Croatia," I replied.

"What are you doing here?" he continued.

"Well, at the moment, I'm making these bracelets," I answered, "but I'm travelling across Andalusia, I found out about this place by pure chance so I decided to visit."

"I see," he sighed pensively as if he was expecting to hear something else.

"Do you happen to know a place where I could set up my tent?" I tried asking him. By his eyes and his body language I concluded that he was harmless, although that wouldn't be my first guess when I saw his appearance. He just seemed completely lost in space and time.

"Hmm, a tent," he gave it a thought, "are you looking for a place to spend the night?"

"Well, yes."

"Maybe I could help you with that, but a bit later," he said, "if you could help me, now."

"How?"

"By giving me 10 Euros, and I'll give you this."

He carefully took a couple of green buds out of his pocket. I noticed a reproaching look from a man passing by. The man was dealing drugs in the middle of the street, in broad daylight, in front of everyone.

"Trust me or not, but I only have ten Euros left in my pocket," I smiled politely, "if I buy it now I won't have anything to eat or drink. Not until I find an ATM and there's none in this village.

"That's true," he agreed, "but at least you'll have something to smoke."

We laughed together from the bottom of our heart. It was the first time I saw him laughing. He still wasn't letting go of the girl, or she didn't seem to want to let go of him.

"Look" he was relaxed, "I, *we*, really need those ten Euros. We need it more than you do, trust me."

For some strange reason I trusted him.

"And, don't worry, tonight you'll have something to eat, something to drink and a place to spend the night," he finished. "I, Manu, promise you that."

He was very proud as he was saying it. I assumed that the man had an intense life behind him, full of adventures and miracles, but it seemed that he hadn't had it easy. Now, he was standing in front of me desperately offering me a few grams of weed for ten Euros.

"There you go," I gave him the last ten Euros I had.

"Thank you very much," he said taking the money clumsily and handing me the stuff at the same time, "meet me in the café in exactly two hours."

"In which one?"

"The only one there is."

They walked away, and I found a tree overlooking Gibraltar, and laid under it. When the sky was clear you could see the African continent from there.

"*Hola*," a lady greeted me, watering the plants in front of her house, while I was walking down the street trying to kill time until I met Manu.

"*Hola*," I greeted her back.

"Mhmm, mhhm," she mumbled something in Spanish.

"*Queee?*" I shouted, letting her know that my Spanish was bad.

She stopped with the watering and approached the fence. She had a dark complexion, long black hair, was dressed in a floral dress and was bare-footed. She looked like a gipsy. She observed me closely putting a large smile on her face.

"Hashish?" She was direct.

I didn't have any money, but I did have some time to kill. And after all that time spent under the tree I felt like meeting someone new. Also, I'd never hung around with a gipsy woman.

I could use the Spanish practice.

"*Puedo probar?*"[13] I managed to put two words into a sentence.

"*Claro*,"[14] she smiled widely showing a gold tooth.

I followed her into a big yard overgrown with plants, among which I recognized only one - Cannabis. She opened the door of her ramshackle wooden cabin letting me go in first.

The room was dark as there was only one lamp lightening the interior. It was a tool shed, in fact, with a bunch of old rusty tools scattered all over the place and there were two men sitting at a table.

I felt their eyes on me, and at the same time my wish to meet new people left me. There were all sorts of things on the table: aluminium foil, scales, bowls, pipes, bongs and – a sharp knife.

The woman started explain something in Spanish, and the two men listened attentively, never stopping with what they were doing: they tore the aluminium foil, folded it in half, and put a yellow-brown powder in the middle. I understood that she'd told them that she'd brought me there to try their hashish, which I would buy afterwards. That was a lie, at least the second half. They offered me a seat and told me to wait for a moment.

One of two men, who appeared to be the boss, the man, the alpha male, took the aluminium foil in his left hand, a lighter in the right, while he was holding some kind of a plastic tube in his mouth. It appeared to be a straw, only bigger and firmer.

He started the lighter and pressed it to the lower part of the foil warming up the powder that was on it. In a matter of few seconds the powder turned into a black liquid, and a smoke appeared which he, ably, with the help of a straw, inhaled deeply. When the black liquid rolled to the other part of the foil he handed the kit to his companion who repeated the same action. So did the gipsy woman.

I observed their actions mesmerized not knowing what I was witnessing. All I knew was that I wasn't feeling very comfortable, and that I was starting to feel a little paranoid. However, at the same time, I was interested in what they were doing and wanted to know how the situation would develop.

"Want some?" the gipsy asked me, noticing my curiosity, offering me

---

[13] May I try?
[14] Of course.

the next round.

"Wha-what's that?" I stammered.

"Heroin," the boss answered smiling at me.

"No, thank you," I refused shyly.

At that moment I felt my paranoia rise to a higher level. I was in a small village in Andalusia, in a shack with three people, heroin addicts. I was surrounded by old tools and there was a giant hunting knife on the table.

I was in fucking *Trainspotting*!

I waited for them to finish their passing game with sweaty palms; I awaited the one thing I'd come there for – the degustation of hash.

"Are there any jobs around here?" I asked them in my broken Spanish, inhaling the first toke, "I could use some money."

"What would you like to do?" the boss asked me.

"It doesn't matter," I replied, "something to help me afford food, drink and a place to stay. And something to smoke."

Everyone laughed. I was starting to relax.

"Maybe we can find you something," the boss feeling rather important mumbled something. I only understood four words: tourists, road, weed and money. I realized his intentions only when he took a piece of paper on which he wrote a price and another one next to it. I'd always been good with numbers.

The man was offering me the job of a drug dealer.

So, I was supposed to be on the streets, talk to the tourists who would come every once in a while to buy some opiates and I would get twenty percent of every deal I made, either in cash or in goods. I could sleep in their yard as long as I worked for them. Or next to the gipsy who kept on checking me out.

I eagerly accepted the offer and told them I would test myself straight away in my new job. The truth was that, in fact, I was only looking for an excuse to leave that place. I wasn't feeling very comfortable in their company.

When we finished the joint, I listened to the final instructions of my new employers and headed to the street. Before that, I tried my luck once again.

"If I would be selling weed and hashish I should know what they're like," I said as I was leaving, "I've tried hashish, can you give me some weed?"

The boss burst into laughter.

"No problem, my friend," he said as he was handing me a considerable amount, "let us know how things are working out, you can always find us here."

I was out on the street. I sat on the curb. I knew that, normally, drug dealers, would hang around the corners, but there was not a single one in the entire village. Luckily, the village was empty. There was not a single tourist with whom I could practice my drug dealing skills.

After half an hour of sitting on the curb, I remembered my appointment with Manu so I went to the only café in the village. Only one waiter worked there, there was one television and only one guest. And not the one I was expecting to find.

I ordered a glass of plain water and sat at a table in the corner. There was a football match on TV; I assumed the World Cup was on. I didn't pay attention to it, but I concentrated on my little black notebook so I could write down all the details of the day.

"Do you want a cigarette?" I looked up and noticed the only guest at the bar standing next to me with an open pack of cigarettes.

"Thank you," I reached for the cigarette introducing myself. I don't usually see any point in smoking cigarettes, but that day was definitely anything but normal.

"What are you doing here?" He went straight to business. He was a man in his mid thirties with a three-day beard and yellow neglected teeth.

"Waiting for a friend," I replied briefly.

"A friend?" He repeated. "What is the name of your friend?"

"Manu." I told the truth, and by the expression on his face I concluded they knew each other.

"And what were you doing with those people an hour ago?" He continued, detective fashion, "I saw you entering their yard."

"They offered me some hashish to buy," I continued in cold blood exhaling the smoke.

"I see," he seemed to understand, "Manu is not coming. But I'm Roni, you can come with me."

I didn't know the reason, but the company of that man made me feel comfortable. I could sense that he was telling the truth, that he wasn't trying to take advantage of me, and most important, I knew that I could trust him.

I got up, and not asking any unnecessary questions, took my backpack, thanked the waiter for the glass of water and followed him.

He stopped after hundred metres, in front of the house of my *Trainspotting* friends, looked me in the eyes, smiled and walked into the yard.

I stopped for a second, but followed him in.

We passed next to the wooden shack I'd been in only recently and entered another house, twenty meters away. And inside there was, no more, no less, Manu.

I didn't understand anything. Which movie was I in? In the past few hours I'd met several people in three different situation and they all appeared to be living in the same yard.

"Hello, my friend," I greeted Manu who only managed to give me an empty look, smile shyly and reach for his lighter, aluminium foil and a plastic straw.

"Don't hold it against him, Manu isn't with us at the moment." Roni tapped me on the shoulder. "Now you can see why he didn't meet you in the bar."

And I saw it. I knew that was where my ten Euros ended up. Still, I couldn't bear a grudge against him.

"Until he's back I can prepare us dinner." He took five potatoes, a big onion, a clove of garlic and a bunch of cherry tomatoes.

He was cooking, I was observing and Manu, still in his own world, was sitting on the bed. Not long after that, just when the dinner was ready, he was awake and joined us at the table. Since we didn't have enough plates we ate straight from the pan in which Roni prepared the food. Perhaps because I hadn't eaten anything that day, or because of the whole atmosphere, it was one of the most delicious meals I'd ever had. We shared food, drink and stories. I spent most of the time listening to their life stories, both happy and unhappy memories, which had brought them to this village in the south of Spain.

Manu arrived in Castellar for the first time in '77. For the past forty years he'd been using all sorts of drugs, and for the past twenty years he was on heroin. In the eighties he spent a lot of time on the Columbia–Germany route: he imported pure cocaine from there and sold it at skyrocketing prices. Once, he only managed to sell 28 grams from a kilo. He used the rest of it himself. But even that was enough to go back for another stash.

Soon, the word got out on the streets of Berlin that Manu was dealing the best coke in the city and the Russian mafia didn't like it very much: they paid him a couple of visits, stole everything he had, threatened him with a knife at his throat, beat him up with baseball bats and left him in that condition to die alone like a dog. He was saved by German doctors, who had given him a medical discharge after months in hospital. He had twelve bolts and three metal plates in his head. It would cause him life-long problems with metal detectors at airports.

Finally, he'd decided to come back to Castellar and stay there where he had old friends who, after all his escapades with cocaine and German hospitals, thought he was dead. All kinds of rumours circulated around the village. There were three versions of his death. And there he was now, pulling through, earning his living by selling weed to tourists while he spent most of his earning on the yellow powder that he got at his next-door neighbour's.

"How does it feel smoking heroin?" I asked him in the morning, still sleepy, as I observed him preparing his morning dose. After our dinner they didn't let me set up my tent, but, instead made an improvised bed, insisting that I spent the night inside.

"What can I say?" he replied, holding the kit in his hands, with the straw swaying in his half-opened mouth, "I cannot sleep without it, I cannot eat, I cannot walk, I cannot live. Heroin controls my life."

I watched him, thinking about his life. What kind of situations must've happened to him to bring him to where he was now, in the middle of a village in the south of Spain with only one thing on his mind, how to get money for another shot that would help him forget.

If my life had played out differently, who knew where I'd be and what I'd be doing. It's possible that I'd be in Paris selling my young body. All in all, only when confronted with situations like that did I realize how lucky I was and that, unlike many others, I'd grown up living in a fairy-tale.

He started the lighter only on the fourth attempt and put it closer to the foil. He stopped for a moment and turned it off. He looked up, gave me a sober look, possibly the only one for that day, and said, "please, remember only one thing. What I'm doing now... Don't ever try it. There is no way out."

I'd just witnessed the best anti-heroin ad ever made. If I ever wanted to try it now, I was sure that it'd never happen.

I went out into the yard and not long after I heard someone asking, "how's business?"

I looked to the left and what scene there was. The Boss from yester-day was standing by a tree, in a T-shirt with his pants around his ankles. He was laughing, with his hands on his hips, and urinating.

"Still nothing," I replied looking him directly in the eyes, "I'm headed for the streets right now to see the situation.

I got out on the street realizing that there was nothing in that village that could surprise me anymore.

The village was dead and there was nothing to do. Since I didn't have any money, and I didn't want to impose myself on the guys during their meals, or work as a drug dealer, it was time for action. I had to get to the civilization and head further east.

I took a walk to the castle, saw a couple of tourists and then I returned to Manu's place. He was sitting in front of his house, playing with the dog.

"I think I'm going to move on today," I told him, "if only I could find a job around here to earn some money to buy food, or if I had a guitar to play around the castle, for tourists..."

He looked at me, went into the house and brought me a guitar with five strings. I took it realizing, surprisingly, that it was well tuned. It sounded great, even without string number two. Manu made me a sign in Spanish to explain to the people that I was from Croatia, that I was travelling and that I needed money for food.

Soy Tommy de Croacia, necesito un poco dinero para comer.
Gracias.

I gave him a hug, being careful not to break any bones in his fragile body, took the guitar and headed towards the castle.

There wasn't a living soul around. That was fine by me, it would give me some time to practice a bit and get attuned. I wasn't much of a singer, and I also wasn't much of a player. I put all my hopes in the sign where people could read something about me and by a small contribution, help a stranger on his Journey.

I placed myself next to the entrance to the castle, put the cardboard sign and a plastic bowl and in front of me and threw in the only coin I had, one Croatian Kuna, and played the first chord. A minor. That was my favourite one.

I had only ten songs in my wide repertoire, and most of them were in Croatian. It wasn't much of a start, but I was hoping that people, if any people should appear, would appreciate my effort despite the language in which I was singing.

I bit my tongue in the awkward conversation,
I don't know why, I don't know why...

With my eyes closed I was playing my favourite song, one that reminded me of...

"*Suerte.*"[15] Just then a man passed by, rustling a plastic bag, throwing a one Euro coin into my bowl.

The feeling was amazing. My chords grew stronger and louder, just like my voice in which you could sense self-assurance. That first coin marked an official beginning to me becoming a street musician. I'd always been one of those people who would look at the street artist and secretly admire their music skills and the courage to stand on a street and give a tiny piece of themselves to passers-by.

One song after another, several tourists appeared, stopping at the entrance of the castle, taking a few photos and reading my sign. Nearly all of them threw a couple of coins into my bowl, either on their way in, or on their way out of the castle. Also, someone gave me a can of juice and a sandwich so I decided to take my first break.

That was it. I was happy and fulfilled. I was giving a piece of myself to passers-by, through the songs I sang, and they were giving me something in return, through their smiles and the coins. That was enough for me.

"Mummy, mummy, look. The man is singing in English." A little girl ran to me, she was perhaps seven or eight, with a cute English accent. She stood in front of me, looked me straight in the eyes for a few seconds, smiled at me, and sat next to me. Her parents simply smiled and went to explore the castle. The little one remained. she had a private concert to listen to.

I sang to her all the songs in English that I knew and enjoyed her presence; she was quiet, innocent and focused like only kids know how to be.

Just because she was the best audience, I took my one Kuna coin and gave it to her.

"This is my lucky coin. Guard it somewhere. If you ever happen to come in my country you can buy a chewing gum with it."

She accepted the coin, looked at me with her dark and deep eyes and gave me the firmest hug in the world. It was a lot firmer than I'd imagined a seven-year-old could give.

The gorgeous little being's name was Nikita. She was from New Zealand and she was travelling with her mum and dad across Spain. I played her another song, and in the meanwhile her parents came back. They took the photo of Nikita and me, threw in a couple of coins in my bowl

---

[15] Good luck.

and left, leaving me with one of my dearest photos and, definitely, one of my favourite experiences from the journey.

I played for an hour more throwing glances at the bowl. I'd made fifteen Euros in two or three hours of playing. Moreover, if you take into consideration that there weren't many people, it was more than excellent. I decided to play for another half an hour and then call it a day.

As I was playing the final songs, slowly starting to feel the fatigue in my left hand, I noticed two girls who were looking around some houses nearby. Suddenly, they sat ten meters away from me listening carefully to my performance and taking a few photos.

They approached me, threw in a few coins in my bowl, introduced themselves and asked me who I was and what I was doing there. I told them that I was travelling, hitchhiking, sleeping in strangers' apartments, and I also told them the story about how I ended up playing guitar in front of a castle in a village on top of a hill in Andalusia.

They were extremely interested in everything I had to say, more than they were interested in my singing.

"We travel across Spain, too," they said, "soon we'll be going home, so if you want to, you can come with us."

"And where is this home of yours?" I wanted to know.

"Bilbao."

"That's on the other part of the country, right?"

"Yup, on the very north, it's a thousand kilometres away from here."

It took me a few minutes to weigh up the offer while the girls did a tour around the castle. Finally, no matter how much I loved saying 'yes' I had to turn them down. I nurtured a feeling that some other important things were waiting for me in Andalusia and, honestly, I didn't feel like going north just because I could. Anyway, it's not that warm in the north and it rains quite often. I thanked the girls for their wonderful offer, played them another song and gave them a hug goodbye.

After a successful day I treated my hosts to some freshly bought groceries and we prepared dinner. The following day I decided to repeat the previous successful day so I took the guitar and went to the same place. On my way to the castle I bumped into a middle-aged couple. They spoke German between them. I greeted them, they greeted me in return, and when I moved away a bit they said something incomprehensible.

"Sorry, what?" I said turning around.

"Would you play something for us?" they asked me politely.

I sat next to them and played two songs for them. They listened to me attentively, and, at the end, I was rewarded with my first applause.

"You're a great singer," they agreed unanimously, "come with us to have a cold beer."

Even though that would probably mean my work-day was over, I accepted their offer. They took me under the arm, and showed me the way to the yard in front of their house. I was surprised to see that their yard wasn't the same one I kept ending up in for the past couple of days.

Cans of beer kept on coming, just like the stories. They told me about the history of the place, about Manu; they warned me about certain people who I should watch out for (one of them was, of course, my Boss) and explained the way they decided whether they liked someone or not.

"You know those machines in the hospital to which sick people are attached?" They asked. "Imagine healthy people attached to them. Those showing signs of life, who are sometimes happy, sometimes sad, who aren't afraid of winning or losing, who give themselves completely to what they do; people whose life line on the screen goes up and down, we love those people. However, those whose line is always flat, we don't love those. They never take chances, they don't stand up to anyone, they're indifferent to what's happening around them, they don't want to experience big failures, or big losses, yet they will never experience great and breath-taking victories."

"Intensity," I commented.

They nodded. We were on the same page. What truly mattered was the passion with which you approached and lived life: were you actually living it or were you just passing by, not having enough time for the details, the small things, the miracles. In that case, you were only a passive observer, instead of being the star of the movie.

After many hours spent together, they offered me a place to sleep, an old hippy van which was no longer in driving condition, although it could still work well as a sleeping cabin.

Two nights in the van and a couple more Euros earned playing the guitar later, I moved on. I arrived in Alhaurín el Grande, on my way there getting four Euros from a driver, and positioned myself in a huge house with a pool surrounded by greenery and luxury. I was planning on staying there for a few days, helping my host with the house chores in exchange for food and accommodation.

The first thing I did was something I had been thinking about over the past four days in the hippy village – I had a shower.

Day 565.

When are you coming home from Spain? It would be great if you could come to our agency once you're back so we could see whether we could help each other somehow. You always hitchhike, you never buy plane tickets?

If you need, let's say, travel insurance, we could be your sponsors and all you have to do is mention us every once and a while, wear our T-shirt, you know how it goes... I'm giving you food for thought, and when you come back we should definitely meet and have a talk!

Maja

Maja was a colleague from the university who was now working in a travel agency.

My new travel-writing project was finally starting to pay off. I replied that we'd definitely meet once I was back, grabbed my backpack and headed for the road.

After a few days in that magnificent house with a pool, I was back on the road heading east. I wanted to visit another place I'd heard amazing stories about, Beneficio, a hippy commune inside of the Alpujarra national park.

It was only one hundred and fifty kilometres away so I planned to get there the very same day, especially since I travelled the first hundred kilometres in two hours. However when, seven hours later, I was still waiting, standing in the same place with the Andalusian sun shining heavily, I started seriously doubting my decision.

"What could the Road have in store for me today, I wonder," I asked, looking at another car passing by. I managed to make two girls in a car smile, which still wasn't enough to make them pull over. Not one car pulled over, not even to ask me where I was headed. Not one. I must've broken some sort of a record.

A screeching of brakes. I looked to the left, a car with two girls in it pulled over just before the highway entrance, made a U-turn. My heart started beating. They were moving towards me, slowing down and rolling down the window.

"Hey," a blond girl in a bathing suit greeted me.

"Hey," I greeted her back, hopeful.

"What are you doing?" the other girl asked me, a brunette wearing the same outfit. "We saw you some five or six hours ago, when we were going to the beach. Now we're coming back. Where are you going?"

"To Beneficio, towards the east," I crossed my fingers, "and you?"

"To Málaga, towards the west," they replied together.

It was an awful feeling, the disappointment, when you were so close, yet so far away. I would've given everything if those two gorgeous ladies were going in my direction.

"Well, so it goes," I said, "thanks for at least pulling over and asking me where I was headed."

They smiled at me, rolled up the window, and went to the roundabout to get back on the highway.

Wait a minute, I thought to myself, it's getting dark and you'll have to spend the night on the beach. There's nobody waiting for you in Beneficio. Maybe you could go with those two to Málaga, even though it's not on your way? If you're lucky, and you often are, they could be registered on the CouchSurfing site.

"Hey, wait!" I shouted, waving them to stop the car, which they did, "do you happen to know of any cheap accommodation in Málaga where I could stay if I went with you? It's getting dark, and I don't feel like sleeping on the beach."

They looked at each other, had a brief talk in Spanish and said, "get in, you're sleeping at our place."

Once again, I was the luckiest man in the world.

I got in the back seat concluding that my face would wrinkle in no time from all the non-stop smiling I was doing at my life situations. I introduced myself to my new friends and they did the same thing.

"We are two students and we have an apartment in the centre of Málaga," Amanda told me, taking something out of her backpack, "that's all you need to know about us for now."

They laughed out loud. Sandra cranked up the volume of the radio and started singing loudly, while, having taken out everything she needed, Amanda started rolling a joint.

So, these two cheerful girls took me to their home, gave me a clean towel and left me alone in the apartment while they went to the supermarket to buy some groceries for dinner.

"I hope you won't mind sleeping on the couch," Amanda said to me after dinner.

"No worries," I told them, "it's in my job description: I travel and sleep on other people's couches."

They took me by the hand, and took me out. We started our evening by listening to a street flamenco singer, continued with roaming around different local bars, and ended up in a salsa club where my girls danced ravishingly in their fluffy dresses.

"I've had enough for tonight," Sandra joined me as I was trying to doze off a bit in the club, "shall we go?"

"Yes." I got up straight away. "What about Amanda?"

"She still feels like dancing," she smiled, "I don't. And you don't either, as I've noticed."

"You've noticed well," I smiled, too, and took her by the hand.

On our way to the apartment she gave me a Spanish lesson. I didn't care much about learning it, but I enjoyed listening to her pronouncing letters 'c' and 'z'. The tip of her tongue nearly touched her upper teeth, puffing out air, at the same time creating a little air bubble and that beautiful sound. I believed she noticed it after I asked her to repeat the word *cerveza* for the fifth time.

She laughed. I found that even more adorable.

"Let's watch a movie so you could learn a bit more Spanish," she suggested as we were entering the apartment. Although I was quite sleepy, barely keeping my eyes open, I followed her to her room, on her bed on which she put the laptop and started a movie by Almodóvar.

We snuggled, pretending that our attention was directed only on the movie.

"I hope your roommate won't mind spending the night on the couch," I said drowsily as I realized that I would be spending the night in their bed.

"Why should she sleep on the couch?" she looked me directly in the eyes while the corners of her mouth and eyes twisted into a smile.

"Say 'cerveza'," I said after a few minutes of silence.

"Cervez..."

Day 567.

"Don't worry, we'll give you a ride," the girls suggested when I told them that I was leaving Málaga, "it's only one hundred kilometres away, and we'd love to see what's going on in Beneficio."

Only a couple of days before, they'd picked me up on the road, hosted me in their apartment, fed me, showed me the city, let me watch them dance salsa, and now they wanted to give me a ride to my next destination.

"If you ever happen to come to Croatia, I'll spoil you just like you've spoilt me." We shared a group hug and got going.

After a short ride, we arrived to Orgiva, followed an unpaved road to Beneficio, parked the car and started searching for the hippy commune situated in the centre of a national park.

We noticed lots of vans, camp-houses, and even a London double-decker from the fifties, redecorated and transformed into a functional home. We spotted a bar with a couple of people who didn't seem to look like hippies. Once in the community, there were no alcohol or drugs allowed, so that bar was the last stop for people to refresh themselves a little with a beer.

The path we were on didn't appear to be part of a national park. It was mostly made of sand and rock, and very difficult to walk on. Still, after we crossed a little creek, the unremarkable path became a forest trail surrounded by greenery.

"We're here," I informed the girls as I spotted the big Indian tepee and two girls wearing rainbow-print dresses and with dread-locks on their heads.

We looked around the tepee, the name of which was Big Lodge and which was, judging by the flyers lying around, the centre of the community and a gathering place. There were people inside playing instruments, sleeping, or smoking joints.

We followed a path uphill, spotted a couple of smaller tepees, some small clay houses, a couple of dogs and playful children, half-naked and naked people doing their everyday chores. Nobody paid attention to us – three curious tourists.

We found a spring where people would go to take their fresh mountain water and a waterfall where the people would wash, using the gush of the water for a real, strong massage.

There was no electricity and no sewers, no television or satellite dishes. All the dwellings were made out of natural materials and didn't have a negative effect on the environment.

The girls helped me set up the tent where I was planning to spend the following few days. I asked for the permission from the people who were living close and they simply laughed, telling me that I could do whatever I pleased.

"Thank you very much for everything, my dearests." I walked my two angels to the exit. "I hope our paths cross again."

We hugged, kissed each other and went our separate ways.

"Got any tobacco?" a blonde man asked me, interrupting my thoughts about the beautiful days I'd just spent in Málaga.

"Got any rolling paper?" I asked him.

He had, I had: the situation was ideal for the two of us to become best friends.

"I've been here for the past eight months." Lukas started telling me his story after we placed ourselves by the forest path, taking out the rolling papers, tobacco and the rest of the stuff we needed. "I live in a cave at the top of the mountain, but I've run out of tobacco so I had to come down here."

"What brought you to Beneficio in the first place?" I wanted to know.

"A search for peace, meditation, isolation," he said. "I got sick of the world in which I'd grown up, so I decided to try out something different. Totally different."

"How is this so different to the outside world?" I liked the role of the questioner. It seemed to me that my collocutor had a lifestyle similar to mine, he had just decided to stay in one place, instead of travelling from one place to another.

"Surroundings, mostly," he said looking somewhere behind me. "Here, look up."

I turned around, noticing a naked female body walk slowly down the path. It belonged to a twenty-something-year-old girl with short brown hair and hazel eyes and full breasts; it was decorated with colourful tattoos that covered her entire left arm and a large part of her back. A beautiful face, a beautiful body, a beautiful scene.

"Out there," he continued as if he hadn't just witnessed the unforgettable scene, "she would be accused of being immoral, or, at least, labelled as a freak, rude or crazy."

"Of course," I said, convinced that someone could make the same conclusion even here if they came with the outside way of thinking.

"And why?" he asked, inhaling the first toke, "she's only naked. She must have a reason for that and it doesn't concern us. She is not doing harm to anyone, and yet, she would be accused because her behaviour doesn't fit the traditional concept. Here, people can bare themselves, both literally and figuratively, without being afraid that someone will judge them or excommunicate them. And when human beings aren't under pressure anymore, aren't afraid of not fitting in anymore, of being judged" he said, passing me the joint, "then they can concentrate on themselves, discover who they are, what they like, where they want to go. Away from the surrounding which imposed those answers upon them, which define them, away from what they thought was defining them."

His story reminded me of the stories I'd heard from Mongoose, told many months before. The need to take a step back, the need for an unknown environment, an environment where you're unknown to the others, an environment where different rules applied. The need for answers that you have to look for yourself, forgetting everything you thought you already knew.

We soon separated. I went to the centre of the action: Big Lodge.

There were fifteen people in the biggest tepee in the village. There was a fire in the centre around which people were sitting or dancing to the rhythm of a djembe, didgeridoo or guitar. One of them got to his feet and started speaking in a weird language, pointing with his finger at everyone gathered around the fire. He seemed to be engaged in black magic in his free time, and throwing evil curses at everyone who didn't pay attention to him. On my left and right, rolled joints and clay pipes kept circulating.

That night, untypically of me, I didn't say a single word. I simply kept observing the tongues of fire, which always had different forms no matter how long the fire burned for. I observed the intoxicating smoke, people and their careless, peaceful movements, the dance of half-naked girls. I observed my inner struggle: there was my common sense on one hand, which was telling me that I was surrounded by freaks, stoned loafers, people who couldn't teach me anything. On the other hand, my present self quite enjoyed where I was, not judging, but simply observing.

And what I noticed was pure simplicity, pure unity of those gathered there, despite the differences. I assumed that none of them were joined by long friendships, but were connected by a strong energy to which I managed to let myself go and, with the rhythm of the drums, feel the magic of the togetherness of my new, unknown family.

The following morning, after waking up in the beautiful forest, surrounded by the chirping of the birds, I went straight to refresh myself: my first shower under a waterfall.

Having found it, I noticed a familiar body standing under it: the gorgeous girl with brown hair and hazel eyes, dressed in the same fashion as the day before; in her colourful tattoos. She was standing under a strong torrent of water rubbing her hair with her fingers and looking towards the sky through her closed eyelids.

A few seconds later, she was done and stepped out of the waterfall, rubbed her eyes, and, as if she could sense my eyes on her, she looked directly to me. Not taking her eyes off of mine, she took a few steps and stopped right next to me. The pointiest part of her body was nearly touching me.

She was shorter than me by a head, and beautiful enough to make everyone lose their head because of her. She put a wide charming smile on her face, raised her right arm and touched the tip of my nose with her index finger.

She stood like that for a second or a two, flashed me another smile and went away.

I stood there for a few moments, waiting for my heart to stop beating heavily so I could carelessly immerse myself in the same gushing water under which she stood a couple of moments before.

I remained there for an eternity, not having to worry that the residents of the camp would have to pay a large water bill the following month. I moved to the other side of the torrent, looked through the water and noticed drops of water playing in the sun, creating a rainbow. I was thinking about the girl with hazel eyes and her soft touch. I was thinking about life and how I was happy that I was living it.

Even though the community was originally founded as a barter society, there were people in Beneficio who had decided to start their own small business so they could afford some privileges of civilization. So, I found a small bakery, a house where they sold cheese made of goat's milk, the same goats living in front of the house, and at the top of the hill I found Benewifio – an Internet café.

Since it was situated in a hippy village, the café itself was decorated in the same fashion: it consisted of a covered bench placed in front of the house of a naked hippy with dreadlocks, a mini laptop and an extension cord connected to two solar panels.

I liked the concept of connecting an alternative lifestyle with a modern one. The fact was that most people live in an extreme way: they either use all the privileges of modern technology, drive cars, use computers and mobile phones, watch television, have a dish washer and washing machine; or, as in this place, they give up completely on civilization, live in harmony with nature, produce their own food and do all the things that machines could easily do instead of them.

Why does the modern world have to give up on living with nature while the alternative lifestyle gives up on technology? Why couldn't we take the best of both worlds and live in harmony with nature, with the help of technological breakthroughs? The happy, naked hippy at the top of the hill, with a small laptop powered by solar energy was a good example of how the things could work out.

"Nice flip-flops," I said to a guy when I climbed down the hill, noticing that we had the same make. He was in the middle of the process of filling a pipe, he just looked up, looked at my feet, smiled gently, and motioned me with his head to join him.

I sat next to him silently, not wanting to interrupt his diligent, solemn and thorough work. He was in a kneeling position, sitting on his heels, with his back straight up breathing synchronized. He was breathing in deeply, as if it was his last breath, and breathing out in the same way, as if he was breathing every bad thing out of his body.

"Bom Shiva," he said with his eyes shut, drawing the pipe nearer to his forehead and then lowering it to his mouth, always with the same concentrated movements.

I took the matches and lit the mixture of tobacco and ganja, which he, keeping the rhythm of breathing, inhaled deeply. A dark smoke came out of him; there was enough of it to fill an entire room, if we happened to be in one. He pressed the pipe to his forehead once again passing it on to me afterwards. I repeated the same actions, but more clumsily.

"Smoking *chillum* is a sacred act," he said shaking the ashes out of the pipe. He took out a stone filter of an unusual form and started cleaning his kit. "Since it is from India, where you will end up one day without doubt, there are rules you should be aware of."

I cocked my ears and closed my eyes. I was feeling the power of the sacred act.

"Bom Shiva is an act of paying respect to Shiva, who is associated with this plant in many legends," he explained calmly. "The respect is shown by pressing the *chillum* to your forehead before the very start. The first time you inhale, you move it to the right side, using your right hand only. You can also move it to the left, but then you have to say Bom Kali, with which you're paying respect to feminine energy."

I was absorbing the information, realizing that I'd never perceived smoking weed as a sacred act. Just like in Amsterdam I'd experienced the medicinal effects of the plant, now I was ready to explore other spheres.

My collocutor and religious master's name was Raya and he was born in England. According to his stories, he'd been travelling for the past eighteen years, spending most of the time in the Far East and he was a regular attendant of Rainbow meetings all over the world. Beneficio was, in fact, a Rainbow village, where the same rules were applied and the same lifestyle was practiced as during the meetings. At the moment, he was elaborating a larger project and gathering people who knew something about ships and wanted to join him.

"Ships?" I asked, "why do you need ships?"

"The Earth is changing" he said convincingly "for the worse. Soon, we'll be witnessing natural disasters like fires, earthquakes, and eruptions. The electromagnetic radiation of the sun is getting stronger, and that's a fact."

"Many won't survive it," he claimed pessimistically. "Still, Africa and South America will be the continents least affected by these changes, that's why I'm gathering people and equipment to be prepared for the transoceanic evacuation in one or two years."

His plan sounded dangerous. I turned my not-judging filter on and listened carefully to his predictions. I even remembered the name of the city that would be the base of his big project. Of course, the chances that everything he'd told me was pure rubbish, were, also, quite high, although I'd leave him 0.1 per cent of a chance that he was right. If his predictions turned out to be true, the rest of us, the 99.9 per cent, would be complete dumbasses.

"And you?" he asked me, "what do you want from life?"

I told him my life story briefly. I told him everything about my life in Zagreb, my huge debt, my first journeys and my plans for the future, which, mainly, included more journeys.

"Now I'm working on becoming a travel writer," I said proudly, "but unlike other travel writers, I will write about something more interesting, different and alternative. And I think people will cherish that."

"So, you don't like the way in which other writers write about their journeys?" He was curious.

"Not really," I confessed. "You usually need a lot of money to travel in that way. It's easy to travel when you have money."

"Ego, my friend," he said, looking deeply into my eyes, "you have a problem with the size of your ego."

"But..." I wanted to defend myself.

"Let me finish," he interrupted me. "You criticize others who simply have a different approach from yours. At the same time, you claim to be alternative, different, that only you are entitled to know the right way, that only you know the truth. You're trying to be better than the others, when, in reality, there shouldn't be any competition. It's a way that will lead you to destruction," he concluded.

I tried to find a way to defend myself against his words.
"Do your thing, in an honest way, the best way you can. Observe others, learn from them, but never think that you're better or greater than someone. The only person you can be better or greater than is yourself. Because you're the only person you know everything about."

He smiled at me, got up and went off in a random direction.

I sat there for quite a while thinking about his words and my reaction. The words of that stranger were strangling me, they were making me nervous, there were making me justify myself, have a debate with myself.

He was right. What is the point of competing with others, of making comparisons with others regarding something I want to do in life? Where did I get the right to think that something that I create will be better? It could only be *mine*. And that was the only thing that mattered.

As it was getting darker, I went back to Big Lodge, to spend another night hanging out with the rest of the village. Everything was just like the night before: there was the fire, people were playing instruments, dancing, smoking. The only thing that was different was that there was a fifty-odd-year-old woman sitting next to me, playing guitar, behind which she was hiding, just like the majority of people in Beneficio, her naked body.

She was fully concentrated as she finger-picked the guitar and hummed a relaxing song. Suddenly, she got up, turned to a group of people and started a monologue.

Since she spoke in Spanish I didn't understand almost anything of what she was saying, but she seemed pretty upset. There was something theatrical in her performance and I was so impressed by the whole scene that I couldn't take my eyes off of her, enjoying a performance of which many Hollywood actors would've been jealous. The movements, words, energy she was emanating; it didn't even matter what she was saying, but the way she was saying it.

"I don't know what that was all about, but it was wonderful," I whispered in her ear when she sat back next to me, puffed out.

She looked me deeply in the eyes and smiled at me.

"Nothing new, I sensed that they didn't like my playing."

"I liked it," I smiled back.

"Then come with me, so we can play in peace." She offered me her hand.

I didn't give it much thought, even though the old me would've thought tons of things: what would the others say seeing me taking a naked woman by the hand, a woman who could be my mother, and leaving the tepee with her? I didn't care about it at that moment, I was free to do whatever I wanted. There was no one who knew me, and even if there was someone, I knew that, there, gossiping, talking behind people's backs and judging weren't the usual activities.

We went out into the night, there wasn't a moon or any other source of light lightening up the sky. I let go of her hand and looked for a flashlight to help us see in the dark.

"Put it away, you won't be needing it," she said softly, stopping in front of me, "just follow me."

I did what she said, put the flashlight away and followed her blindly. Literally. It was pitch dark. Even though my pupils were dilated, there was no help in the middle of the forest. She was a few steps ahead of me, saying a word or two every now and then so that I knew which way to go. I was wondering how it was possible for her to see, while I didn't, but I was also wondering where she was taking me. Excitement, curiosity, and even fear were growing stronger within me, especially when I heard the murmur of the water and realized that we'd have to cross over a bridge in order to get to the other side.

"Don't be afraid," she said simply, and with nonchalance crossed over to the other side.

I was listening closely to the murmur of the water, which appeared very loud when compared to the silence of the night; it only increased my awe of the bridge I had to cross over. It still was still pitch dark.

I felt the wooden bridge with my right foot and unbelievably slowly, millimetre by millimetre, I engaged in the adventure of crossing over. The bridge was, in fact, made of two thick branches placed next to each other with a small gap in the middle. I thought of the movies in which people crossed the suspension bridges. I was shaking, feeling the adrenaline rushing through my body.

A zillion moments later I was on the other side.

I kept on following the Forest Woman, all the way to her home. She lit a candle, which illuminated the entire space in which we found ourselves. In the centre of the forest there were a few thick blankets that served as a bed, and from the branches hung three sheets that served as walls, while there was a framed photo hanging from a tree. And that was it. A few pillows, a guitar and a few pieces of clothes, which she was apparently using. Only not today.

We both played a few songs, after which we started talking. I liked her: her way of pronouncing the words, the confidence that accompanied her words, the impulsiveness with which she changed the subject. She was crazy. However, since the smile never left her face and since I could see the spark in her eyes, I couldn't do anything else, but enjoy her company.

After all the wonderful stories, mostly hers, we lay down on the blankets in the middle of her home, covered ourselves with a couple of more blankets and pressed ourselves against each other, after which we – fell asleep.

The following morning Forest Woman was gone. I looked up to the sky, stretched and laughed at my situation. I'd spent the night in the forest, in someone's home made of a few blankets and sheets with a photo on the tree, next to an insane woman who could be my mother.

Life is full of wonders.

Leaving her home I was faced with the big challenge from the previous night once again: the dangerous wooden bridge, which I'd crossed shaking. I burst into laughter. Although the previous night it was extremely difficult to cross it, in broad daylight I realized the simplicity of the situation. I could've literally stepped over the bridge, without the slightest effort.

Soon, I ran into Lukas, who showed me the place where people would leave clothes, shoes or anything they don't need any more. Free exchange of goods. He told me that you couldn't find remains of food, garbage or pollution of any kind, which was something the civilized world has to face every day.

"People here produce their own food, or they buy it on Thursday at the market in Orgiva; they take what the sellers don't sell that day," he said, "so, they cherish it as pure gold, which is the reason why nothing is thrown away."

"As opposed to Western countries, where nearly half of the food produced is wasted," I added.

"That's right," he confirmed. "Besides, everyone here builds their own homes, makes their own furniture and the things they need every day so they respect it and do not throw it away so easily."

"As opposed to Western countries, where people change and buy things depending on the current fashion," I added once again.

"Bingo," he laughed. "Here, if it's possible to recycle something or re-use it, then people do so. And as far as the pollution is concerned, our lives depend on a couple of sources of water – if there was no water in Beneficio, there would be no us. Everyone here is educated about the importance of protecting the environment because it's the only home we've got. Also, we know that the environment will treat us the same way we treat it."

"That's something modern society keeps on forgetting, because people's lives are so detached from Mother Nature," I carried on.

"There is practically no trade here, no richness or poverty, people don't need new mobile phones, kids don't need the newest toys," he was finishing, "you'll find pure life and self-sustainability here."

A few moments later, we bumped into my companion of the previous night. That is, she bumped into us. She was a bit more decent then the previous night: she was wearing her panties.

"I would like us to sleep together tonight." She was straightforward, not paying attention to Lukas.

"Well, we...we did sleep together," I stammered, smiling reluctantly, "right next to each other."

"Yes, but..." she smiled seductively.

Soon, I was with Lukas climbing to the top of the mountain, to the cave where he resided. I wanted to see his home, but I also used the opportunity to escape from my new fan.

I had a wonderful night with her. Still, a thought kept coming back to me: she was old enough to be my mother. And that put me off thinking that there could be something more between us than simply hanging out. Was I discriminating against her because of her age? If she'd been twenty years younger, most likely I couldn't have stayed away from her and her craziness, nudity and smiles.

After an hour of climbing, we arrived at the cave. It seemed to be carved into a cliff on the top of the mountain and you could tell that people had been using it as a residence for quite a while.

"This cave doesn't belong to anyone," Lukas told me, "nobody owns it, or owns the rights to it. Except nature. If somebody wants to live there, they're free to. The only thing that matters is that the person who is already in it should not be disturbed; however, if it's free, it's free for someone to move in."

"It would be wonderful to live here," I was thinking out loud.

"If you want to, it's yours for tonight," he said, "either way, I was planning to sleep at a friend's place."

And so I became the Cave man.

I took out a big mattress in front of the cave entrance, very close to the brink of the cliff. I enjoyed the clouds, as I wasn't able to enjoy the stars; the only thing that was disrupting the atmosphere were the sounds coming from Orgiva nearby. I assumed the Spanish national football team had beaten someone in the World Cup.

Even though a couple of years before, I had been a strong supporter of Dinamo Zagreb and the Croatian national football team, the idea that at that moment, nearly all Spanish people were riveted to television screens, drunk with celebration and happiness because the team that represented their country had had a sporting success seemed pointless to me now. So far away.

I remembered the moment when I decided to stop watching sports: a match against Turkey, 2008. After the most shocking end to a match ever, I couldn't bring myself to stop crying. For the weeks that followed, I felt nausea in my stomach. All because of the failure of a group of eleven well-paid players. They made me feel bad, depressed.

I found a recipe in those days: if they win, I'd celebrate with them. If they lose, which was more often, I wouldn't get too upset. A perfect compromise. The world was full of things that we could let affect our feelings and our mood. I didn't want sports to have that privilege.

I survived the night on the cliff and the following day headed off to the northeast.

Don't judge. Don't compare. Don't categorize.

Those were the lessons I was taking with me from the little hippy village situated in the mountains of Alpujarra. Also, I would take the need for compromise between two extremes. I would live life somewhere in-between, not label myself as a hippy or an urban man, or in any other way. Explore all the worlds that there were to explore, decide what I liked in each and take only the best from them.

Follow my own path, away from all categories, labels, groups. Be myself.

Day 577.

"We screwed it up," I heard the driver talking to his co-driver, "it's a diesel after all."

I was on the highway somewhere between Granada and Alicante when the car that had pulled over just a few moments before, started spewing dark smoke, as if it was a cousin of that tepee from Beneficio that everyone would gather around at night. The two men had filled the tank with gasoline instead of diesel.

Somehow we managed to drag ourselves to a car mechanic where we spent a few hours, after which they gave me a ride to a small village of a couple of hundred inhabitants. I spent a couple more hours on the road waiting for one of the few cars and their drivers to have mercy on me and give me a ride to Alicante: I had a flight scheduled the following day to Venice, sponsored by my father.

During the hours spent there, I was the main attraction in the village. People approached me to have a talk with me, children offered me lemonade and old people observed me from their balconies. The only ones who didn't find me interesting were the drivers, the only ones whose attention I really needed.

"Are you hungry?" a couple of kids asked me, after I realized I was having sunstroke from all that standing on the road.

"Yes." I didn't hesitate.

"Come with us."

They took me to a mandarin tree and helped me pick a few mandarins, which were still a little unripe, but still delicious. They showed me the way to the spring where I could fill my empty bottle, and, since it was getting dark, they took me to an abandoned house, telling me that I could spend the night there and, that, if I wanted to, I could play football with them, which I accepted whole-leggedly.

They accompanied me to my mattress and my sleeping bag telling me not to leave the place the following morning before meeting them.

The following morning each of them had a plastic bag with all sorts of gifts: cookies, fruit, sandwiches, juices, just in case I needed them. They left me speechless. They even offered me some of their savings so I could buy a bus ticket to Alicante, which I couldn't accept, no matter how grateful I was.

We said goodbye and took a photo together. I left them the cardboard

I used for hitchhiking and playing in front of the castle, and arrived at the airport the same day. A few hours later, I was in Venice, with Sarah, and a few days after that in Zagreb.

Another adventure ended successfully.

But this time, I wasn't alone. At least not in the virtual world. I had a couple of hundred of people with me, following me on my new Facebook page. I received words of support from complete strangers, who'd come across my page because of recommendations from their friends, or by pure chance. They congratulated me on my courage, encouraged me to continue with what I was doing and some of them even asked me whether I had the intention of bringing someone along with me – they were willing to join me.

And, when I returned home, that was what filled me with positive energy. Unlike my first journey across Europe, after which I felt completely drained, the situation was different. I had a plan. An idea I was working on.

All I had to do now was improve it.

I took my marketing book out, not to study for my last exam, but to see what my next step was. I needed more attention from the media, more people following my page. I needed sponsors.

I had thirty-five thousand good reasons for it.

Day 794.

"The man I was staying with in that village," I went on, "found me a guitar, so I played it and earned some money, along with a few sodas and sandwiches."

I could've said to her that I was working as a drug dealer. Or at least that I was trying to.

The public dug those wow-stories. The little peculiar details that could be combined in their heads creating an entire scenario that, in most cases, was completely unrelated to reality. And travellers, once they found themselves in the situations like that, would smile mysteriously and let their imaginations run free. Or, they would even add fuel to the fire and make up a few tiny details.

There was a thin line between personal growth, growing mature and wisdom that the Road can bring you on the one hand, and boosting your own ego on the other. A very thin line indeed. I had crossed the line a couple of times when I thought that I was so smart and superior just because I had a bunch of kilometres and interesting stories behind me - a couple of illegal actions, broken hearts and nights under the starry sky.

At the same time, I was perhaps forgetting the most important lesson a person can learn when travelling: the one about being modest. I was perhaps forgetting that we are small, irrelevant, just passing by. Forgetting that each and every one of us has a story of their own and a life path, and that no one's more important or better than anyone else.

I'm a traveller, you know. I'm a hitchhiker. The world is my home. That was only a different way of saying, I'm so great and there's no one like me. I mean, I'm one of a kind. So unique.

Just like I was telling my colleagues from the university that I was a stockbroker. I thought that I was defined by it, that this fact showed others people who I was, and that people should know how to treat me, how to respect me. I thought that I was the man.

Just as, one day, I would say proudly: I'm a writer, you know.

"So, do you travel on your own?" Daniela asked me.
"Yes, I do..."

I guessed she wasn't interested in hearing my story about a sheep which accompanied me on my journey in Andalusia and which even got a name, Maria Juana del Campo. The choice of the name came from her cute face, soft smile, half-open eyes and the things we consumed that night.

I'd given up on travel companions a long time before, after my first trip to Amsterdam. I knew that most of my friends didn't want to travel the way I was doing it, or if they did want to I was sure they'd drop out at the last minute. And convincing and adapting were tiring for me. Still, at one time, I'd given it a try.

"...well, apart from my second to last journey," I added, "One day I created my Facebook page..."

Day 501.

One day, as I was considering either a career as a gigolo or a bank robber, when preparing for my last exam, I received an e-mail:

Hi Tomislav,

We're soon organizing a conference on travelling, which will take place in Zagreb. The travellers/presenters will do a ten-minute presentation on any subject related to travelling. Our aim is to get the attention of the audience (especially the young ones) and make them begin travelling and make them realize that in order to start travelling all you need is a bit of will and courage.
We would love someone to do a presentation on CouchSurfing, so let us know if you could do it.
The timetable of the presentations and the list of the presenters are in the attachment.

Regards!

I read the e-mail once again, threw a quick glance at the list of presenters and saw some familiar names, and one in particular, Hrvoje Šalković, a.k.a. Shale, the writer whose intercom I buzzed on ages ago.

You can count me in.

How could I refuse the offer to do a presentation on CS, which had taught me so much and which was responsible for all the changes in my life over the past few years? Moreover, I'd be with people who'd started travelling when I was at elementary school. Maybe Shale wouldn't refuse my invitation for a beer this time?

During the following few days all I could think of was this presentation. I invested hours and hours in choosing photos, arranging slides, trying to think of witty jokes to make my audience laugh, coming up with questions to hand out to my friends in the audience so they could ask them at the end of the presentation, just in case no one else had any.

I invited my parents to the conference and, talking to them, I finally revealed to them that during all my journeys I'd travelled almost exclusively by hitchhiking. My dad, sticking to his principles, which didn't agree with my way of travelling or living in general, refused to come, while my mom took a seat in the third row and waited for the conference to begin.

In the meanwhile, I tried to come up with a plan to approach Shale, who was talking to Maja, my acquaintance from the university, and one of the fellow presenters. I chose the right moment, sneaked up on them, greeted Maja and turned to Shale:

"Tomislav, pleased to meet you."

"Hi, I'm Shale."

"I know, I rang on your intercom a few months ago."

"That was you?" he was surprised, but in a good mood, "haha, sorry, dude, I had some problems with my girlfriend, and, also, I found it a bit unusual to go grab a beer with a stranger."

"No worries" I forgave him instantly, "we'll have another chance to do it."

"We can do it after the conference."

"Sure."

He was my favourite writer again.

I sat and listened to the lecturers talking about their adventures, stating the most beautiful and most memorable places they'd been to, explaining why and how they'd been travelling. Even though everyone was talking about the same thing, travelling, each of them had a particular style. They flew in planes, went on foot, sailed, visited places other people hadn't. They described their journeys in books, newspaper articles, reports, on blogs, in documentaries, or they caught the colours of the world through the lenses of their cameras. In that way, they financed their lifestyle and their adventures.

I listened, I learnt and thought about it. It wouldn't be a bad thing to do what they'd been doing: travel and, at the same time, earn some money. Instead of going abroad and paying off my debt by doing a monotonous job, after finishing university, maybe I could do what I adored – travel and be paid for it.

It was my turn to talk. I got up and talked about my experiences with CouchSurfing, both as a host and as a guest. I mentioned a couple of stories from the road and in ten minutes I tried to depict my way of travelling and show how affordable it actually was. By the interested expression on the faces of the people in the audience and by the questions they asked at the end of my presentation I concluded I had managed to do it.

That night, just like every other night I had spent in my parent's home,

I went out on the balcony, leaned on the railing and thought about the day that was behind me.

On one hand, I gave a presentation along with some of the famous Croatian travellers and I sensed that I could be doing the same thing, I could turn my passion – travelling – into a source of income. True, it took them years of experience to stand out of the mass of people who did a similar thing, and start selling books, earn money from writing reports, shoot documentaries, sell photos. I didn't have that much time, or talent to do such things.

On other hand, that day I realized that I was different from them in one thing. I had, what economics would call the competence advantage. All those travel writers, photographers and directors travelled using, more or less, conventional methods for which they, usually, needed a lot of money. I didn't need much money for travelling and that was exactly what people could find interesting: they could find out more about a way of travelling in which you don't need a lot of money, find out how to hitchhike, sleep on other people's couches, play guitar on the street, volunteer, etc.

Everyone wants to travel, but no one has the money. In other words, everyone would want to know how it's possible to travel without spending money.

The idea was born.

However, in order to put the idea into practice, I needed a channel to reach people. Television, newspapers, radio – no one was crazy enough to give money to a nameless kid who suddenly decided to travel and document the whole thing. Anyway, I was sure that many people had already approached them with similar ideas. I needed a direct way to reach my audience, and if possible, for free.
The Internet!

Everyone is online these days. People read internet portals instead of newspapers, blogs instead of books, download movies instead of renting them, hang out in the world of social networks instead of having a cup of coffee in the real world.

"My travel-writing texts were published because I had a different tactic from other travel writers," Shale told me that day. "I offered free texts to magazines, and in exchange I'd include a few words about the sponsor, a photo of their logo on a T-shirt and stuff like that. Others criticized me for doing that because people used to earn money from their texts, not from sponsorship."

I got back to the room and turned on my computer. I visited Shale's Facebook page and explored it a bit. In the past few months, the man had gathered a couple thousand followers, and FB was an excellent platform from which to launch short stories, photos, videos.

Facebook and I, in fact, had one thing in common: we were dedicated to many things at the same time, but never to one thing completely. I liked that. I wasn't a writer or a photographer, but when I posted a few photos from my first journey around Europe and left a brief description, a few friends confessed to me that they felt as if they were travelling with me.

I looked at my marketing book, which I should've already started reading more thoroughly, and simply put it into the drawer so it wouldn't distract me in my biggest marketing project – creating my Facebook page.

First, I had to come up with a name.

It needed to be something everyone would understand, in English, with a story related to it. Something easy to remember.

Of course, I laughed, remembering the name I was given in a park in Berlin. Thomas Love. And since the page was supposed to be about my adventures, the solution was logical: *Thomas Love's adventures.* It even had a double meaning. It could mean Tomislav's adventures, since the pronunciation was similar to the way my name is pronounced; and it could also mean Thomas loves adventures, if you disregarded the apostrophe.

I spent the entire night posting photos from my previous journeys and leaving descriptions in Croatian and English. At the same time, I was experiencing everything once again and thinking about how it would be nice to go back on the road. Maybe I should? After all, if I was working on becoming a travel writer, I should travel, shouldn't I? Perhaps that could be my first business move.

I took my shabby map of Europe and made a fast decision – Spain. I should've explored it better the first time, so this could be my new chance. I'd pick the date the following day and go.

Feeling genuinely happy, I fell asleep.

Dearest wall in our rented apartment.

One of the first hitchhiking experiences - coming back from Sofia.

Arriving to Ričice, my mum's village.

Ričice

Conversation with God.

Drunk ride.

Serial killer van.

Breakfast in bed in Hamburg.

Amsterdam

Lola's puppies.

Desperate hitchhiking, on the way to Paris.

Kind driver.

Most beautiful moment in Paris.

Above Nice.

Towards Zürich.

One bearded hitchhiker.

Venice.

Four leaf clover.

Punta Umbria

The crew.

Happy driver.

Starry starry night.

Castellar de la Frontera.

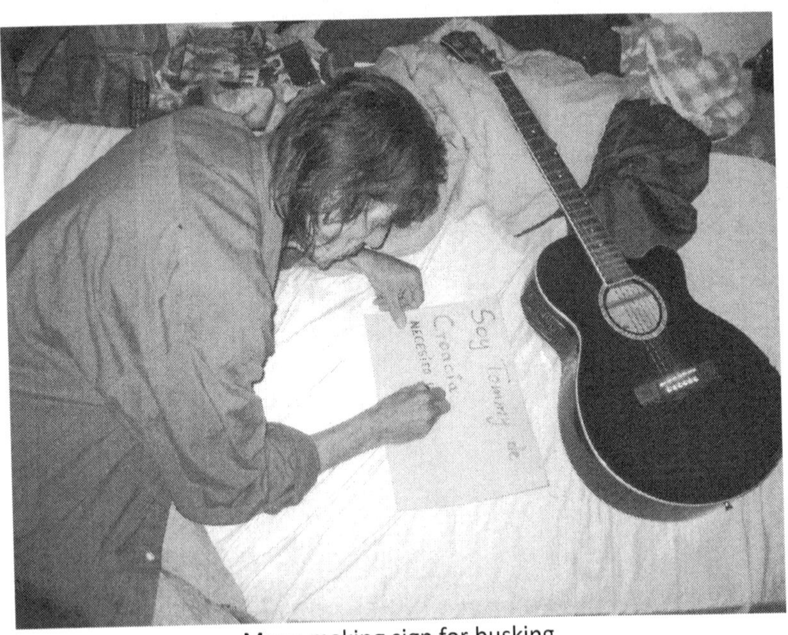

Manu making sign for busking.

Nikita and I.

Amanda and Sandra.

Big Lodge

On the way to the cave.

Last bed in Andalusia.

My little friends bringing gifts.

Shale and I.

Day 794.

The CS presentation, a beer with Shale (who was in the studio with me and who'd suggested to the TV editors that they invite me as a guest) and the creation of my FB page, those were the main reasons for me sitting in front of Daniela and answering her questions. If it hadn't been for that day I'd still have my journeys, but no one would have heard about them.

I used to wonder why I cared so much about people hearing about my journeys. Shouldn't I just travel and keep it to myself, ignore the Internet, media appearances, sponsors? Wouldn't I, in that way, be a truer traveller? A real traveller, whose ego isn't boosted when he sees an article about himself on an Internet portal; one who doesn't post photos on their Facebook page looking forward to every 'like'; who's cool and who doesn't care about superficial and trivial things.

However, in the end, I always manage to convince myself that I have done the right thing. Even if I disregarded the biggest reason why I even started considering promoting my journeys – that huge debt, I was proud of the path I'd chosen.

My stories, published online and shared with those interested in them, had touched at least one person. And if I managed to make someone stop for a while, try to change something in his or her life, start travelling, I'd be extremely happy because of it. I knew what it felt like to be on the other side. I had been on an entirely different life path, but I'd changed the course of my life because of the stories I heard from other people. They showed me a better life path, a real one, a more exciting one. Reading different texts online, hanging out with Nina, talking to many CSers: it all had a great influence on my life.

And now, in a slightly different way, without entering into people's living rooms, I was doing the same thing. I was inspiring people to fantasize. And I was quite proud of myself.

I was finally living my life the way I wanted to live it and I was presenting it in public without any difficulty. The very fact that I was capable of publicizing my life convinced me that I was leading a good one; and that I shouldn't be ashamed of my actions. It was simply me. And I liked who I was, whether the others liked it or not – but judging by all the 'likes', it appeared that I wasn't the only one liking me.

Naturally, there was always that thin line I should have in mind, simply in order not to start loving myself too much.

"People slowly started joining my Facebook page," I was answering Daniela, "and some of them even showed interest in joining me on my journeys. So, one day, it occurred to me that I could make it possible for them to experience a similar journey; that's why I organized a hitchhiking race from Zagreb to Istanbul..."

Day 611.

"Shale was a guest the other day on *Dobro jutro, Hrvatska*[16], maybe you should send them an e-mail," Tea suggested me one afternoon, in a local pub, after her day at the office.

The first thing I did after my return from Andalusia was visit the travel agency that offered me a sponsorship while I was in Spain; maybe I could even make a deal with them. As soon as Maja and Tea the owner, invited me for a beer, I knew that we'd get along well. We made a general agreement: we would promote ourselves on our Facebook pages. Once I was on a new adventure, they would give me their T-shirt and a travel insurance policy, in exchange for a few photos with the T-shirt with their logo on the back.

Fair enough.

The other thing I did was register myself on forum.hr, the biggest and the most visited Croatian online forum in order to find a way to use it for self-promotion. It was widely read and registration was free – exactly what I needed. However, I needed some kind of approach. If I was to push people into liking my FB page or browsing through photos from my journeys, it could backfire. I knew that I would get on people's nerves and that, out of principle, they wouldn't give me a thumbs up.

I scrolled down to the sub-forum Tourism and spent a few days exploring it. The essence of the forum was that it was made of people who had registered many years before, as soon someone new showed up and started being smart, they would cut them out quickly, in the same way as when a person joins any new group and starts acting smart. They were lucky if they didn't get beaten up. As far as the forum was concerned, they would get virtually beaten up, but it wasn't any less painful.

I started a new topic called "travelling on an extremely-tight budget" in which I asked other members what their ways of travelling cheaply were. I described my way of travelling, ending the post with an inconspicuous signature – a link to my FB page.

I pressed ENTER and crossed my fingers.

When the second person who left a comment responded that he had taken a look at my page and my photos and concluded that I had a similar style to that of a guy from the movie *Into The Wild*, I knew that I'd hit the

---

[16] 'Good morning, Croatia', a morning TV show.

right spot.

The elders of the forum initiated a discussion about my travelling style, I replied, humbly, trying not to brag about my actions or claim that my style was better than someone else's. After all, it wasn't *my* style, it was the style of a bunch of people; all I did was present it to the general public through the Internet. I endured a couple of virtual attacks by people who accused me of abusing the generosity of my hosts, but the best part was that I didn't have to defend myself alone, other members, seeing that I wasn't trying to impose my story blatantly and that I wasn't assaulting other travelling styles, sided with me.

The number of 'likes' on FB kept on growing every day.

The third step was contacting my high-school friend who worked as a journalist for 24sata[17]. She arranged an interview with their newspaper: they took a photo of me with my guitar, backpack and a road map and I ended up on the front cover.

I was quite satisfied with what I'd done: there were now over one thousand people following my adventures. And more importantly, I did it all for free. The messages of support kept on arriving, as did messages in which people expressed their wish to join me on my next journey. Honestly, it was something I didn't want to do. It was one thing to travel on your own, but a whole different thing to take someone with you, especially a stranger.

I found out about the fourth step only this morning when Tea suggested that I contact the people from HRT's[18] morning show.

"Do you think they would invite me?" I asked feeling a bit scared.

"There's only one way to find out," she encouraged me.

I finished my beer and went straight home to type an e-mail.

Dear Sir or Madam,

I am writing to you to put forward a suggestion for a report which you could do in your "Dobro jutro, Hrvatska" show.

My name is Tomislav, I am a graduate student at the Faculty of Economics in Zagreb, and when I do not have any exams to study for, I travel in a quite special way, on a budget of couple of dollars a day. I get around by hitchhiking, I sleep in my tent or at other people's places

---

[17] '24 hours', a Croatian daily newspaper group.
[18] Croatian national television.

whom I come across CouchSurfing; I play guitar on the street and similar things.

During my last year of studies I went on a couple of journeys, visited twenty countries and more than fifty cities and covered more than twelve thousand kilometres using my thumb.

I also have a page on Facebook with more than one thousand three hundred followers, where I put stories and photos from my journeys.

I stood for a moment to see what I'd written.

It was missing something. When I tell them where I've been and what I've done I should also add something about my future plans, a new project, something that will occupy the viewers' attention.

I know.

I am organizing a hitchhiking race, the first one in our area, where everyone who wants to can apply and the application and the participation will be completely free.

I took a road map of Europe out of the closet and chose the route I found the most interesting.

The race will take place from Zagreb to Istanbul, through Belgrade, Skopje, Thessaloniki and Xanthi. I believe your audience will be interested in the event and it could maybe even encourage them to join it and be a part of a big, adventurous journey.

I'm available for any possible questions.

Regards,

Tomislav Perko

That could be a hit – two birds with one stone. My being on the television show would bring me a great deal of media attention, and I would also make it possible for the people who wanted to join me to actually do so.

The following day there was a reply in my inbox.

Dear Tomislav,

The way you travel is very interesting, but in order to talk in more detail about your experiences and a possible collaboration, I suggest that you send us a number in which we could contact you.

We do reports on travelling on Mondays and we can make ar-rangements to host you in our show. In any case, we will keep in touch.

Kind regards, B.

That was it. I was going to be on television.

Day 617.

My early morning interview went very well, and after that I was richer by a couple of hundred 'likes' on Facebook; I also received tons of messages and e-mails from people interested in the adventure to Istanbul. I replied to all of them telling them to stay tuned to my Facebook page so they could see all the information in time, and that the beginning of the race was planned for the beginning of October, after the university exam session.

All I had to do now was organize the whole thing.

"I hope you won't have to use them," Tea joked, promising travel insurance policies for all the race participants.

"Fuck, I didn't even think about it," I was worried. "What if something happens to someone during the race? Even though the journey will be free, since the participants would hitchhike and couchsurf, if something bad happens, we know who'll be responsible."

That thought bothered me for the rest of the day until I decided to stop thinking about it. Think positive. That was the lesson the Road had taught me. I hoped it wouldn't let me down when I needed it most.

During the following weeks I received a bunch of e-mails, which I stored for the day when I would make everything public. There were more than thirty people interested in the race. That wasn't exactly the best news ever: where would I find a place to stay for so many people in those cities? Where would so many people hitchhike on all those roads and highways?

Every day I wrote requests to CS communities in the cities we would be passing through. The responses were great. When I explained to them what we were planning to do, that a bunch of people would participate in a hitchhiking race from Zagreb to Istanbul, they were very excited and ready to help. We found four or five hosts in every city, but only one in Skopje.

Finally, one evening, I sat down and put it all on a paper. I had to explain the rules of the race. So, I sat down and started writing:

> *Since the date of the beginning of the race is coming closer it's high time I gave you the detailed information about the whole project of the hitchhiking race from Zagreb to Istanbul so that each and every one of*

you can prepare yourselves!

INFORMATION

Everyone who wants to participate in the race has to:
1. Send me an e-mail with their full name and surname, address, date of birth, and a link to their CS profile (those who don't have one can set one up);
2. Know that this isn't a regular journey, but an adventure in which we'll be hitchhiking, couchsurfing, and doing other unpredictable things. Everyone is responsible for themselves;
3. Have a passport that is valid for at least half a year;
4. Have some money for food or any other emergency, and a mobile phone with enough credit on it;
5. Treat the people who you'll be travelling, driving and staying with respectfully;
6. Be honest and fair – this is a race, but there won't be a prize; our aim is cooperation, not competition.

The route hasn't been 100% defined yet, but it should be: Belgrade – Skopje – Thessaloniki – Xanthi – Istanbul – Sofia – Zagreb.

The estimated duration of the journey is three weeks. As far as the hitchhiking is concerned we'll be divided in male-female pairs. You can find yourselves a partner before we start the race, but if you don't have one, we'll find one for you by random choice.

RULES OF THE GAME

Maybe the word 'rules' isn't the best choice, but here I'm giving you a few suggestions of how the whole thing should be on the road:

1. I will repeat once again: you have to treat other hitchhikers, drivers and hosts nicely. I don't doubt that you will. If any problem arises, we'll sit down together and discuss someone's inappropriate behaviour. I won't be a judge, we'll always make all the decisions together.
2. The aim of the race is to arrive in the city as soon as possible; HOWEVER, it's advisable to experience something during each stage of the race. In every city participants will be awarded points, and at

the finish line we'll announce the winner, who will get – nothing.

3. As far as cheating is concerned, not only is it allowed, it is very advisable! So, do whatever it is in your power to arrive at your destination. If you happen to have a friend who will follow you in a car and drive you from one city to the other, go for it. You'll get the most points, but also nicknames like 'pussy', 'crook' and other similar names to that. The point of the whole thing is to have fun, without something bad happening to anyone. This is your journey; no one will tell you how to travel.

4. You have to be fair when counting the points. Each person will measure their own time getting from one city to the next and the things they experienced on their way there. No one will ask for proof, we'll take your word for it.

You will get points if:

- you're the fastest group, +5 points, every group that arrives after you gets a point less;
- you have the funniest/craziest story to tell, +3 points;
- you end up in a village, spend the night beside the road and never even get to the destination, +5 points;
- share a breakfast/lunch/dinner with your driver, +2 points;
- you have the most interesting souvenir from the journey, +1 point;
- take the best photo on the journey, +1 point;
- help your driver repair the car, +2 points;
- spend the night with the person who gave you a ride (no sex), +4 points;
- spend the night with the person who gave you a ride (sex included), +3 points;
- a Ferrari or a Porsche, or something like that pulls over, +3 points;
- if the driver lets you drive the car, +2 points (+5 if the car is a Ferrari or a Porsche);
- if the driver gives you a ride directly to the house of your host, +2 points.

If someone rapes you, murders you, or if you're left without a kidney during the race, you'll be the automatic winner!

We will take the points away from you if you:

- use public transport (bus, train or taxi), -5 points (you can only use public transportation when you leave a city and look for a place to hitchhike);
- pay for accommodation (hostel, hotel, private accommodation), -3 points;
- don't fasten your seat belt, -20 points;
- discuss politics, religion or football with drivers/hosts, -3 points;
- walk along the highway, -3 points;
- drink or smoke weed with your driver, -2 points (but, who cares?);
- leave your partner while hitchhiking, -15 points and a kick in the ass from the other participants.

We'll count the points each time we arrive in a city. Our plan is to organize meetings with the hosts the first night we arrive in a certain city, where we'll have a drink and talk about the day that'll be behind us.

Once you're on the road, you'll be given the address and a phone number of your CS host, whom you'll contact when you're close in order to make all the necessary agreements. You'll most likely go with them to their apartment, leave your things, take a shower and join the others at the gathering.

At the end of the journey, the person spending the smallest amount of money will be awarded 50 points. The second will get 40 points, the next one 30, and so on... The winner will be the person with the most points! That person can brag to their friends and neighbours over a drink. Good luck!

I closed the laptop and shut my eyes. This could be one awesome journey.

Day 623.

"Are you online?" a chat box popped up.

The reaction of my body to her presence, even though she was many, many miles away from me, didn't stop surprising me. My heart started beating heavily, a smile appeared on my face, my brain was instantly trying to figure out why she was writing to me.

"Yes," I replied briefly. Of course I wanted to shower her with questions to find out why she hadn't been writing to me, why she was writing now, whether she was thinking about me... However, I restrained myself.

"In a few months I'll be in India!" she wrote.

"Great!" I typed following the rhythm of my heart, "a friend has just invited me to her wedding in Bangladesh."

"Perhaps I could join you."

I sat back and fixed my eyes to the screen. Was she aware of the effect her words had on me? Why couldn't I understand her words as a pure, random, innocent joke? Why was I instantly considering the possibility of going to India straight from Istanbul?

"In a few weeks I'll be heading for Istanbul, along with other people," I decided to ignore her last words.

"Sounds like quite an adventure!" she replied.

"Still, if I win the lottery, I'll see you at a wedding in a couple of months," I couldn't resist writing.

"Just let me know and I'll be there."

"Copycat."

Day 646.

Hey T.

I think I have big news for you. We'll have to meet for a drink ASAP to talk about something. I may have found you a sponsor.
Call me.

Iva

Iva was a girl I'd met in the juice bar where I had been working, and who had heard about my adventures from a friend.

"Look…" she started our friend-business partners meeting the following morning, over a freshly squeezed carrot, apple and pear juice, "I work for a PR agency and it crossed my mind that I could suggest you to a client who might be interested in what you're doing."

"Yeees?" I cocked my ears, "which client, if I may know?"

"Of course," she smiled, "but not a word to anyone, at least for now. It's MasterCard."

"Wow!" I smiled back to her, "not bad."

"Nothing is for certain now, but I think we stand a chance," she continued, "it's up to us to suggest a project to them that they won't be able to refuse."

"Hmmm," I started thinking, and after a few seconds I had it. "How does Bangladesh sound to you?"

"Bangladesh?" she was surprised, "what will you do in Bangladesh?"

"A girl who stayed at my place a year ago, is getting married in Bangladesh," I explained. "The wedding will last for five days and there will be a couple of thousand guests. The colours, the feast and stuff like that. Besides, do you know anyone who's been to Bangladesh? Sponsors might really like it, because if I managed to use their credit card *there*, at the other end of the world, then people would conclude it could be used anywhere."

"You're right," she said, "what do you think, how much money would you need?"

"Honestly, I have no idea," I replied, "I usually spend a small amount of money on my travels, but here, we're talking about a journey to another part of the world."

"Okay, okay, let's write it all down," she put away her juice and started writing. "A plane ticket, some pocket money, travel insurance; what else do you need?"

"Well..." I gave it a minute to think about it, "maybe it wouldn't be a bad thing to have a good camera and a small laptop to take notes, edit photos and stuff like that."

"I'll see about it," she underlined what she had written down. "Do you have a blog where you publish your stories?"

"For now, I only have a Facebook page," I said, "but I could start writing a blog."

"Great. The more channels through which you can reach the public the merrier for the sponsors."

"Of course," I nodded, "and if I get a camera and a laptop, I could create my own YouTube channel and upload short videos."

"Great. Oh, another thing," she smiled, "I studied your Facebook page last night and saw that cute little sheep of yours - Maria Juana."

"Ah," I said dreamily, remembering my little sheep.

"Yeah, I found her cute, too," she said, "but you do realize that MasterCard is a serious company and that you should avoid writing about things that her name reminds me of?"

"Of course," I repeated, although I didn't like the idea of compromising. Still, as I remembered my debt I decided to keep my mouth shut.

"Great." She finished her juice. "I'll let you know when I put it all on paper and present it to our clients."

"Thank you very much." I hugged her and walked her out of the bar. "I think I've just come up with an idea for the name of the project."

"Yes?"

"Yes." I was proud. "What do you think of *No cash in Bangladesh*?"

"Awesome!" she yelled and left.

If that worked... I didn't even want to think about it. I would've got myself a big sponsor and, maybe even more important, I would be only a few hundred kilometres away from India.

Day 668.

I got the news while we were in Skopje, our second hitchhiking stop on our way to Istanbul. It was, in fact, a sad day.

All fifteen participants were in the same house, with three hosts, and we'd just had the winner of our race. The rule of someone getting raped, killed or losing a kidney came into effect.

Tanja, the craziest participant in the race, who brought her dog Nina and her parrot Čiči, was climbing down the stairs when she started crying.

"Čiči," she sobbed holding a small lifeless creature in her hands.

Everyone stopped talking. Each and every one of us, like a true family, gave her a hug and a few words of consolation.

"That was the happiest parrot in the world," someone said.

"Definitely the first parrot-hitchhiker," another person said.

"It'll be remembered as the winner of the first hitchhiking race in this area"

We managed to put a smile on her face. She was glad we were there for her.

And seeing everybody gathered around, I felt warmth in my heart. I saw a group of people brought together by the Road and the fact that they were travelling together. A group of people who hadn't known each other before we started the journey, but who were now, a couple of days later, behaving like friends. As a true family.

I had already sensed that at our first stop, in Belgrade.

In Zagreb, the night before we left, we met for a drink and split ourselves into random male-female pairs. I handed out sheets with contact numbers of the hosts in the cities we'd be passing through and with the rules of hitchhiking.

There were three foreigners in the group and people from all over Croatia. Only half of us had already had some experience with CS and only three people had some experience hitchhiking outside Croatia. The youngest participant, Sanjin, was only nineteen and this was his first time he had crossed a border or used a passport.

He was the one who, after arriving in Belgrade, told me something after which I already knew that our journey would be extremely successful.

"Dude, somewhere around Slavonski Brod, Dalibor and I were picked up by two beautiful girls from Zagreb and during the whole ride the folk music didn't stop playing in the car," he was talking in the cute island dialect, by his haircut and his pierced nose you could tell that he was into punk subculture, "and, yet, it didn't bother me, which was weird because usually I can't stand things like folk music."

I knew exactly what he was talking about.

"However, in the end, we did screw them up," he smiled deviously, "when we were crossing the border we told them that we had loads of drugs with us so they should pretend that they didn't know anything. Ha ha, you should see how pale they suddenly were."

Sanjin wasn't the only one who already had an interesting story after the first four hundred kilometres. Tanja, along with Nina and Čiči, got a ride in a Bentley worth a quarter of a million of dollars, Joanna and Evan ended up eating *burek* with their drivers, while Nina (not the dog) and I ran into a driver who had been a bodyguard for the Serbian president during the war.

Ingrid and Igor, after a rough start, arrived at the first stop after a 14-hour delay. We ran to hug them as soon as we saw them, thrilled to see them; especially I, who kept thinking that something might have happened to them.

I now better understood my mother's feelings from when I was on the road.

The remaining three couples arrived in Belgrade with normal stories. Ana (a serious business woman who had told her mom that she would travel by bus and who is in Kirgizstan at the moment of writing this book, in the middle of a hitchhiking adventure from Zagreb to Bora Bora) and Jasmin, as well as Pamela and Mario, needed only one lift to get to Belgrade, while Marina and Alex's drivers liked the two of them so much that they left them in front of the house of their host in Belgrade.

Our CS friends prepared us an excellent welcome meeting the

first night. We were placed at four different addresses, and our hosts organized a party at a great restaurant in our honour, and made sure that during the following few days we were on all possible lists for free entrance to Belgrade clubs.

It showed that the warnings we'd been given before going to Serbia were just empty words. Everyone we encountered treated us like royals: our drivers, hosts, people we stopped on the road asking for directions, and the waiters who served us delicious food and drinks. There was no talk of the horrors of the war, differences or grudges, only about new friendships and the similarities between us, even though there was a border separating us.

After being brought closer through our stay in Skopje - sharing one bathroom and the floors of the kitchen and living room when it was time to sleep - everything went smoothly. We did a bit of sightseeing: Macedonian, Greek, Turkish cities, on our own or in the company of our hosts. We tasted the local specialties, both food and drink, played and sang with the street artists, shared hugs, wrote messages of peace and love with colourful chalk in the main squares, and accidentally ended up in a theatre when we wanted to find shelter from the rain. We drove in a hearse, with different smugglers, with Albanian mobsters and many drivers shared food and drink, sometimes even money, with us.

Each participant in the race experienced it in a different way, but no one regretted being part of it. They were thrilled to have discovered a new way of travelling, hitchhiking and couchsurfing, and their hosts too, people who welcomed them as long lost friends.

I was the only one who appeared to be somewhere else, with my thoughts on my upcoming Bangladesh adventure.

Day 699.

"I'm coming to Bangladesh!" I sent her an e-mail as soon as the contract with MasterCard was singed and the plane ticket bought. "Are you still interested in keeping me company at the wedding?"

"I don't think it'll be possible; according to my visa for India I can only enter the country once."
That was a cold shower.

"Well, maybe I could make a short stop in India?" I suggested. "What are the chances of us meeting there?"

"Don't come to India only because of me." She kept on ripping me apart. "But, if you happen to be in India at the same time as me, the chances for us meeting are very high – 99.9%."

I knew it wouldn't happen. That 0.1 % was saying quite a lot.

Day 794.

"A hitchhiking race?" Daniela repeated, "so, who was the fastest to make it to the finish line, who won?"

Everybody kept on asking me the same thing, as if it really mattered, as if it mattered to make it to the finish line. What mattered was what happened on our way to the finish line.
Still, it was my fault, too. No one had forced me to call the journey a race. It's natural for people to expect a race to have a winner, although being a winner isn't anything that special. Winners are alone in their success, surrounded by losers, and they're looking for someone who can understand them, someone with whom they can share their success, their joy, their excitement.
Competition, competition, competition. Always the same story, from our birth to our death. The world would be a much prettier place if instead competing with each other, people would simply cooperate.

"Actually, I didn't want the race to have a competitive aspect," I said, "you could even get extra points if you ended up in a village, slept out in the open and stuff like that. Those are the moments you cherish the most at the end of a journey, the ones you remember the most. Travelling would be awfully tedious if everything went according to plan. The whole adventure of moving, the getting from point A to point B would be ruined. We would be left with only one half of the experience: the one you experience in the destination itself."
"Are those experiences the reason why you travel the way you do?"
"Well, since I don't have any money I basically don't have any other option," I continued. "If I had money perhaps I'd be staying at hotels, eating in restaurants. In that sense, the only journey that was different was my last one, the one to Bangladesh..."

Day 732.

"If you ever want to feel like a movie star, go to Bangladesh", was the quotation I'd come across just as I was in the middle of my preparation for the trip to that country: from taking vaccination against different diseases I could catch there to hitchhiking to the Netherlands and back in order to go to the embassy of Bangladesh so they would issue me the tourist visa for Croatian citizens.

When I was flying to Dhaka, the capital of a country twice as big as Croatia but with an impressive number of citizens – 160 million, I discovered the story behind that quotation. I was the only Caucasian in the plane: everyone was watching me. When we touched down and I got out of plane at an airport enclosed by barbed wire and military men with machine-guns in their hands, I realized that I had just entered a totally different world.

I put my small backpack on since I'd lost my big one somewhere on the Zagreb-Zürich-Barcelona-Doha-Dhaka route and, with a new camera around my neck, started exploring my first destination outside Europe.

The road leading to the city was packed with small, green vehicles called CNG's (the name indicated their fuel, compressed natural gas), also known as tuk-tuks or moto-taxies; overcrowded buses with bumps on all sides; personal cars which kept on honking irritatingly every few seconds; and pedestrians who kept on running over the road playing all brave, but really they were playing with their lives.

When I arrived in the suburbs, the scenes I was surrounded by became even more memorable: motor vehicles were now replaced by rickshaws, while car horns were replaced by the sound of rickshaw bells. There was a small improvised food stand or a tea-serving stand at every corner; electric cables connecting the electric pillars created inseparable nodes; stray dogs and their faeces dominated the side streets; and every now and then you could easily see scenes like a six-year-old lifting a barrel full of trash, at least twice as big as he was, and shaking out its content into another barrel and digging through the trash in search of something valuable.

'Don't feel sorry for us, we're happy with what we have' seemed to be the words that I read in the eyes of the passers-by and from the smiles of the children dressed in rags playing in the muddy streets and posing readily for a few photos. 'If you've come here to be sad, then you better go back to where you've come from.'

I decided to take their advice.

I felt good in the role of a photographer, so I tried to catch reality through the lens of the camera, no emotions involved; just the reality that wasn't similar to anything I'd ever seen before. I gave up my negative thoughts, I no longer felt that I'd come to a place where I didn't belong, I gave up the instinct to sit on the sidewalk and start crying over the destiny of those people, and I stopped listening to the voice that was telling me to take off the camera and to give it to a passer-by who could sell it and with the money earned, feed his four-member family for an entire year.

I decided to try to fit in with the locals, just as on every journey before. Be one of them. A local, not a tourist.

I knew that it wasn't going to be an easy mission in a place like this.

Hey Thomas,

We're downtown, around the University, finishing our school assignment and observing the celebration for the Victory day. We'll be back tonight. Feel at home and feel free to take a nap in the back room, everything is set up. If you need anything, call us.

Christy, Keith and Matt

That was the note waiting for me on the door of my hosts, three Americans who had been teaching English in Dhaka for several months. Besides them and my friend Samai ,who would be getting married in ten days, I didn't know anyone else in the country. Also, I didn't have any idea where I would go after Dhaka.

All I knew was that I didn't want to spend much time in someone's apartment. So, I dialled the number they left on the note and headed for the University.

I sat on a three-wheel bicycle, got myself comfortable, and watched a local with a frail build pedal unstoppably, manoeuvring skilfully through the obstructed streets. If I thought that the streets were dangerous on my way from the airport, being an actual participant in the traffic was a whole new experience. Noisy CNG's were rushing from all directions, fearless busses, cars with front and back steel bumpers to minimize the damage, which, in the chaos that governed the streets of Dhaka, would eventually occur - it was only a matter of time.

A couple of months before, during my stay in Istanbul, I heard a saying: *If you can drive in Istanbul, you can drive in any city in the world.* I pictured the author of that saying getting into a car in the capital of Bangladesh and after the first few metres starting to sob.

If Dhaka has fifteen million inhabitants, I believed that day there were at least ten million of them on the streets. Green flags with a red circle in the middle flew everywhere, people wore the jerseys of their national football team, their faces coloured green. They were celebrating Victory Day, the anniversary of liberation from the Pakistani regime. I still couldn't spot a single Caucasian on the streets.

"How am I supposed to find those three with all this chaos?" I wondered as I was approaching the University and giving my chauffer 100 taka (approximately 1 Euro) for his half-hour pedalling. Among the thousands of people I noticed a commotion in an area where a curious mass of people gathered: I wanted to fit in so I joined them.

I expected to see Bollywood superstars, but instead I was facing – my hosts!

"Ha ha, welcome to Bangladesh," Keith said, referring to the chaos around him, "what a great day to be here."

I met Matt and Christy and joined them in answering questions to the curious crowd. Where are you from? What's your name? Do you like Bangladesh? Literally, there wasn't a moment where someone didn't ask us a question accompanied by a handshake with a local who was brave enough to attack us with so many questions.

They were so simple, nice and curious. Each and every one of them.

Until they became a bit annoying since not even two hours later they didn't stop following us wherever we went and asking the same questions. So, in order not to get mad with them we chose a smarter way out – going back home.

"Uh, that was intense," Matt sighed once we got into a bus that had a wooden floor. "During all the months spent here we've never experienced anything like this. I hope it hasn't been overwhelming for you."

"No, on the contrary," I said, "most of the time I like being the centre of the attention. It's written in the stars."

"Ha ha, then you'll love it here," Christy added.

I laughed and looked through the dirty window at the street. The river of people kept on flowing down the streets, coming from all directions, while the lights of the vehicles illuminated the faces of the children who, with their parents being absent, slept in cardboard boxes at the corner of the street. I could smell smog, burning and poverty in the air.

The smile vanished from my face.

Day 735.

I was in the bus for the old part of Dhaka when I spotted an interesting detail on the bus driving next to us. There was an irregular downward line under every window, as if someone had painted a yellow-brown line using a thick brush from every second or third window. No matter how hard I thought about it I couldn't discover the origin of those lines.

And then a woman riding in the bus revealed the secret. She leaned through the window and – threw up, leaving an identical mark to those I'd noticed earlier on. No one in the bus blinked.

"It happens quite often," a man sitting next to me told me as he noticed me observing the situation, "women aren't very good in standing the heat in the bus. And if you take into consideration the fact that we're in Bangladesh, they're probably pregnant."

Having said that he laughed and I joined him.

"Nurislam, nice to meet you," he offered me his hand.

"Tomislav." We shook hands.

"Tom-Islam?" his eyes were wide with surprise.

"You could say it like that," I accepted my new name readily.

He started asking me all those questions I was accustomed to in Dhaka, and I answered.

"Let me be your guide around Dhaka," he suggested as we were getting closer to our stop, "I could show you some interesting places that you wouldn't be able to see on your own."

He took me by the hand (not literally, even though it wasn't a rare thing to see two men holding hands on the streets of Dhaka) and we went to the river Buriganga, which served as a transport platform for more than a million people every day. In addition to being one of the busiest rivers in the world, it was also one of the most polluted.

"This is the poorer part of the city," he began explaining as we crossed to the other bank of the river, the southern part of the city, in a wooden boat that reminded me of Venetian gondolas.

I didn't have any reason not to believe him. The soil was completely covered with all sorts of trash, the amount of which was so great that the sand that was hiding beneath could barely be seen under all that paper, plastic and God-knows-what other materials. It stank.

The only clean surface was a small football field where half-naked and bare-foot children were kicking around something that looked like a football. Their laughter and happiness in such surroundings seemed quite surreal.

We walked around a shipyard, found our way through the muddy alleys between the shacks where numerous families lived, crossed over wooden bridges that overhung a liquid that couldn't possibly be called a river and, finally, ended up in a textile factory.

I already knew that Bangladesh was the country with possibly the cheapest manual labour in the world and that, consequently, large brands moved their production facilities here, where the income from the textile industry was probably the biggest of all branches of industry. I'd heard about the inhumane working conditions – now I was there, in the hot spot, ready to see it for myself.

The first thing that caught my attention was the great number of women and children, mostly teenagers, working there. The working rooms usually had no windows, and the workers sat in uncomfortable chairs or even on the concrete floor. The fabric was scattered all over the room and you were left with the impression that no job could be done there. In one corner of the room I noticed two women who used the space under the sewing machines as a place to take a rest. They would take a nap between two shifts.

"It's the factory of a friend of mine," Nurislam said proudly, "the working conditions are great, the quality is top-class and the workers are satisfied."

I took another look around the dark room, lit by a couple of lamps, and calculated that there was one worker per square metre, doing their job without lifting their heads.

I wondered what a factory with worse working conditions looked like.

"Everyone works eight hours a day here and they have one hour off for a lunch break," he said as if he was reading my mind. "Many employers force their workers to work twelve hours a day and they pay them the minimum wage imposed by the government.

"And that would be?" I asked.

"Thirty nine dollars," he said, "a month."

"What about the children?" I wanted to know, wondering how anyone could survive with monthly wages so low, even if they did live in one of the poorest countries in the world that was, at the same time, one of the cheapest countries in the world. "Why aren't they at school?"

"They aren't at school because they have to feed their families," he said as if it was the most normal thing in the world for nine-year-olds to work, whatever the reason for that might be. "Employers like younger workers because their sight is better, they're handier and they complain less."

Now I could finally understand the happiness of those kids from the playground. Even a dirty and stinky environment was better than this one, dark and exploitative; unfortunately this was necessary for many of them, young and old, healthy and sick alike because they all had to find a way to maintain their families.

Leaving the factory I was thinking about the poverty circle in which those people were trapped. On one hand, rich companies from rich countries, in order to increase their profit, move the manufacturing facilities to countries where they can pay workers less money. In order to give these companies the lowest operating expenses possible the governments of these under-developed countries embrace them whole-heartedly, making it easier for them to enter the market by offering them different tax benefits and less rigid control of safety conditions, health insurance and so on. The workers, on the other hand, are grateful to have jobs because living in a small country with more than 160 million people, one cannot choose what to do. That is the reason why they keep their mouths shut, accept all the conditions so that the companies are satisfied, so that corrupt governments are pleased, and so that rich Caucasians from other parts of the world can buy a T-shirt for $9.99, made in Bangladesh.

Consumers form part of the poverty circle, too. Even if they are aware of the whole situation, if they boycott products made in under-developed countries they would be doing anything but good: if no one bought their products, they would lose their jobs and have no place to go. If the government raised the minimum wage and increased the responsibilities of the companies, which would then have to take care of the safety and welfare of each worker, the company would only move their facilities to another country, justifying their actions by increased operating expenses. So, the only ones who would suffer would be the workers.

Damn money.

Nurislam and I visited his four-member family, who live in a three-room apartment that they share with two other families. They had one room and half of another, a large wooden bed, and a bathroom that they shared with the other tenants. They shared their lunch with me and a few kind words, after which I returned to my hosts.

I wanted to run away from that city desperately, from the filth, noise and misery. I felt helpless simply observing everything without a solution to change things for the better. Since I'd promised myself, and the others, that I wouldn't feel sorry for them I had to do something else.

"I have a week left until the wedding in Dhaka," I told my Americans that night, "do you have any suggestion; where could I spend the time while waiting?"

"You could visit the amazing national parks," Christy suggested, "but, I'm afraid you can only do that if you go through a tourist agency: you have to book in advance and the package tours may be expensive, which you wouldn't like very much."

"What if I visited those places on my own?" I tried to make a compromise.

"It's not allowed," Keith said, "there are Bengal tigers everywhere; on average, they kill a man every three days; and there is a lot of kidnapping and organ selling."

"Wonderful," my face darkened. "What is your favourite place in Bangladesh of the places you've visited in these past few months, where you don't have to go with someone and where you won't lose a kidney?"

They remained silent for a moment, exchanges looks and then answered together:

"Kushtia."

Day 736.

One of the most terrifying experiences of my life was behind me: a bus ride in Bangladesh.

I gave up hitchhiking when I realized that there was no point in trying to explain to the locals what a white man was doing by the road with his thumb stuck out. All locals, no matter how poor they were, paid for transportation. I didn't see any reason why I shouldn't follow their example.

Everything was okay as we were leaving Dhaka, but once we got onto the highway the horror started: avoiding pedestrians and rickshaws moving close to the curb, overtaking other buses somewhat slower than ours, zig-zagging to avoid accidents just at the last second and, the cherry at the top of the cake, overtaking a bus, which was overtaking another bus, while rickshaws and cars coming from the opposite direction had to move to the dusty part of the road to save their lives.

I was the only one on the bus who considered this driving style dangerous. The driver whistled nonchalantly and maintained a rhythm with the bus horn while the other passengers didn't seem to pay much attention to what was going on: they talked among themselves or slept with their mouths wide open. Every now and then a woman threw up through the window, with her vomit probably hitting an innocent passer-by.

I followed their example and hid myself behind the seat in order not to be able to see what was going on in the traffic. That was the only way to survive: don't look, believe in the driver and in his sixth sense.

"Don't be scared of their hospitality," Keith advised me when talking about the people I was going to visit in Kushtia. He gave me the phone number of one of them and explained how to find him. "When you get out at the bus stop, take a rickshaw and head for the Lalon Shah temple. Once you get there, give him a call. Abohelito is the only one who speaks English, but that shouldn't worry you."

"Welcome," Abohelito, my new best friend and translator, greeted me in his bad English. "This is Boss."

I shook hands with a proud man with a dark moustache on his equally dark Bangladeshi face, dressed in a big brown blanket and the traditional *lungi*, a large colourful piece of fabric similar to the Western long skirt. He held my hand in his unusually long and, smiling shyly, said something.

"What did he say?" I asked Abohelito.

"He said that you have unbelievably soft hands," he replied.

We all laughed and went to the office.

The office was a colourful two-floor building, full of empty rooms that would supposedly soon be transformed into the headquarters of the Boss's company. He owned fields where he grew all sorts of fruits and vegetables, many shops with clothes, musical instruments, souvenirs; he had more than a thousand workers. They led me to a room that had some pieces of furniture and told me that it was mine. There was a large mattress on the floor covered with clean sheets and warm blanket. Their big eyes were wide open waiting for my reaction. When I smiled widely and put the backpack next to what was, given the situation, possibly the most luxurious bed ever, they shouted a couple of words as a sign of approval.

I joined them in the other room where a bunch of people were sitting or kneeling on the mats, which covered the concrete floor, waiting to meet one of the rare strangers in their village.

I shook hands with each and every one of them and sat between Abohelito and the Boss, feeling the curious eyes of the people gathered there on me. A few of them held strange instruments in their hands and waited patiently.

Boss took a one-stringed instrument made of some sort of a pumpkin and two pieces of bamboo between which the string was placed, and played the first note with his index finger: that marked the beginning of the concert.

"These are the famous Baul musicians," Abohelito whispered, "all the songs you'll be hearing are played in honour of one of the holiest man in this area, Lalon Shah, who is buried here, in Kushtia."

He translated the lyrics for me: there was a lot of mockery of nationalism, social division, hierarchy, castes and racism. Lalon sounded like a man who should be followed and even now, after few hundred years, songs should be sung in his honour.

People who weren't singing or playing had two functions. One group was in charge of serving food and drinks, while the second group prepared a mixture of a familiar green plant and dried tobacco and put it in *chillum,* which I already knew from my trip to the south of Spain, to the hippy village.

I neglected the musician and delicious food for a while and concentrated on observing a new way of preparing *chillum*. They used a small wooden board and a small knife with which they chopped a small ball made of ganja and dried tobacco leaves. When the mixture was done they took dried coconut, took out a few threads out of it, burnt them and put them in the *chillum* which they afterwards pressed it to their forehead, dedicated it to Lalon and inhaled through a thin layer of fabric.

Chillums were passed from one person to another, the music grew more intense and louder and the food even more delicious. People got up, raised their hands up in the air shouting the timeless verses, issuing an invitation to the celebration of life and joy.

Boss gave me his instrument, after which the others practically fell into rapture. I awkwardly touched the string with my index finger and with every note that I got right I felt as if I had scored in a match in the Champions League. I felt special, as if I had found my long lost family, like so many times before.

Even though we had different skin colour, and our religions, clothing style, language and way of smoking were different, we were still like brothers in every possible sense of the word. I'd hugged more people during that evening than on a regular night out in Zagreb with friends when we would get drunk. Men there weren't afraid of another man's touch or hug, something that was so wonderfully brotherly.

"It's a gift for you," Boss gesticulated when I tried to return to him the instrument he'd lent to me.

"*Donnobad,*"[19] I replied with the only word I'd learnt, bowing my head as a sign of respect.

"*Ektara,*" he said pointing to the instrument and letting me know its name.

I nodded, gave him another look to show my gratefulness and went to my comfortable room to take a rest from the impressive day that was behind me. Abohelito accompanied me to my room, checking if I needed anything else.

"No, thank you," I said for the zillionth time that day and shook his hand.

"Wow," his eyes opened widely, "Boss was right, you really do have soft hands."

---

[19] Thank you.

Day 739.

I snuck out of my small room, watching that no one would notice me, and took a left turn when I got out on the street having decided to spend at least part of the day in peace in quiet, in the company of me, myself and I.

I hadn't had a single moment of peace since I arrived to Kushtia. Keith was right, I was a bit scared by their hospitality. At the beginning of the each day one of my friends would enter my room with a washbowl full of water, which they used to wash my hands, and a tray full of fresh fruit, a couple of *rotis*[20], some kind of a soup and delicious and fat sweets, all of which he would watch me eat. After breakfast we would go for a walk through the village or on the Boss's estate; they gave me a few *lungis* and a *gamcha*, a thick piece of fabric that could be used as a handkerchief, towel, scarf or as a headband, as gifts. Wherever we went we prepared *chillum* and we prepared so many of them that for the first time in my life I actually had too much. From the early morning, during the day, until the night I always had someone next to me, even when I had to go to the toilet there was always someone standing a few meters away from me, watching and taking care that everything was alright, making sure that at least I had water since there wasn't any toilet paper.

They were really kind and friendly, they never allowed me to pay for anything, but still, after a few days of this royal treatment I wanted to be on my own. Since I knew that I wouldn't be able to explain that to them I decided to sneak out and do all the explaining after.

I started walking to the village Shilaidaha, which apart from Lalon's tomb in Kushtia, was the main tourist attraction in that part of the country. There was the estate of Rabindranath Tagore, the first Asian Nobel prize winner whose literary opus was strongly influenced by Baul musicians. In fact Tagore had a big role in spreading the teaching of Lalon Shah around the world.

Halfway there I hopped into a rickshaw and played the avoiding games. Just as my driver skilfully avoided other vehicles, I, similarly, avoided the aroma of his body, which was carried by the wind straight into my nostrils.

I observed the greenery around me, rice fields and hardworking work-

---

[20] Traditional flatbread.

ers in them, banana trees and their large leaves, palm trees, small lakes where women washed their clothes, kids who were pushing bike tires with a stick on the dusty roads, cow dung drying in the morning sun and then being used as fuel.

Those beautiful villages were the birthplace of many workers in the textile factories I'd seen a few days before when visiting the slums of Dhaka. They left their villages and moved to the larger cities, they left the lifestyle of their ancestors, everything, so they could search for a (better paid) job so they could feed their extended families.

Anyway, life surrounded by that greenery appeared much more natural, healthier and happier than that in Dhaka. However, even those areas were affected by sadness and misery, especially when during the rainy season the rivers were swollen, the cattle was killed, the crops ruined, something that deeply impacted the lives of those people who depended on a couple of gardens and heads of cattle.

Tourism could maybe fix the situation a little, if a conscientious and sustainable approach was applied – said the student of economics speaking from within me. Judging by the experience so far and the absence of foreigners, it was no wonder one of the tourist slogans was, "Come to Bangladesh before the tourists do".

I walked around Tagore's beautiful estate and went back to my hosts, who were about to alarm the whole village because of my unexpected absence.

Just like every other day, we occupied a room in a village shack and enjoyed the evening beside the bonfire, intoxicating aromas, the sounds of the *ektara*, the *dotara*[21] and a couple of drums. Abohelito wasn't with us so my communication with the others was based on my well-practiced body gestures.

"*Shotto bol, shupothe chol, ore amar mon – il*"[22] a grey old man was whispering the words; he seemed to be the wisest, the most experienced and the most respected one.

He pronounced the last two-letter word slightly louder than the previous verses. The room appeared to be filled with an invisible energy, everybody and everything kept quiet, even the crackling of the fire.

As soon as he pronounced the word, he looked at me intensely as if he was trying to tell me something. Without thinking, without hesitation

---

[21] A traditional instrument.
[22] Bengali: 'Tell the truth and follow the right path'.

I repeated after him, a bit louder, "Il".

I discerned the smile in his eyes and the silence of the people who were waiting for the continuation with great tension.

"IL," the old man said once again, louder than me.

"IIIL," I replied a little louder, not paying attention to the others, hypnotized by the intense look in his eyes.

"IIIIIIL!" the whole room shook, and shivers ran down my spine.

"IIIIIIIIL!" I shouted as loud as I could, having taken a deep breath, with the every atom of my body.

We didn't stop looking each other. He kept quiet. He touched me with his right hand, lowered his head, looked at the ground and said one of the rare words that I knew:

"Guru."

A murmur ran around the room and the people gathered there made quiet comments while the old man started preparing *chillum*. For some reason, my whole body was trembling. I was shivering, although I was right next to the fire.

"Guru," the old man repeated, offering me the clay pipe with his right hand, lighting it with a match.

I pressed it to my forehead, pronounced Lalon's name and inhaled like never before.

"Could you explain to me what has just happened?" I asked Abohelito, who joined us later and who listened carefully to the others telling him what had happened.

"'Il' is a word that refers to a deity," he began, obviously very excited about something. "Sometimes we use it when we speak to Lalon, or we use it in an important conversation, as a confirmation of a Holy word. It's hard to explain, but for the old man you've passed some kind of an initiation, which is a part of our tradition."

"An initiation?"

"Yes," he explained happily, "the old man is convinced that Lalon himself sent you as his messenger and that the life of a Teacher lies ahead of you; he is convinced that we could all learn from you."

"I'm not that sure about that," I said, blushing slightly.

"You don't have to be," he smiled, "you continue with your life they way you've planned, everything will turn out to be just the way it's supposed to."

That same evening, the old man told me another prophecy, after seeing me taking two bananas joined together as if they were Siamese twins from a bowl full of bananas.

"You'll return to Kushtia, many years from now," Abohelito was translating, "in the company of your wife and twin sons."

I laughed out loud, just like everyone else. The old man was on a roll.

"Tell him that I'll be back even before," I said to Abohelito, sensing a strong connection with those people from a small village in Bangladesh.

The following day, after the breakfast, they took me by the hand and led me to a nearby river: the legend said that Lalon Shah had been found in it floating in a basket. They dressed me in a *lungi* after which I had a ritual bath.

Half of the village gathered around to witness the whole event, approving loudly.

Day 741.

"Hi," a skinny guy approached me when I came back from my piss-break, at a station on another horror ride from Kushtia to Dhaka (I was going back for my friend Samai's wedding), "what's your name?"

That was how every conversation in Bangladesh started, no exceptions. After a while I came to the conclusion that the people of Bangladesh had made a secret pact a long time before about the rules of communicating with the rare strangers they might bump into. They have all the questions they want to ask prepared in advance.

"My name is Tomislam, I come from Croatia, I'm a student of economics and I really like Bangladesh," I said at once, knowing that I'd already answered the following three questions. I observed his face wondering whether he had any other question or if he'd be confused by my answers.

"I would be very pleased if you come with me and my friends for tea when we arrive in Dhaka," he finally said hopefully, "and if you don't have a place to stay, you can sleep at my place."

Since I had a few days until the wedding, and my American hosts were out of town, I accepted the offer, moved to my new friend Jewel's seat and continued my return to Dhaka.

His friends were waiting for us in front of a street stand where they spent most of their time. They, just like me, were students and were fluent in English. They were dressed in jeans and T-shirts, which meant that their financial situation was a bit better than most other citizens; however, they did have one thing in common with the rest of the country – they observed me with admiration. I still had some difficulties absorbing the fact that the only reason for that was the colour of my skin.

When a couple of people gathered in a street nearby and started playing badminton I joined them readily. It was the first time for me to be participating in an activity where I was equal to the others. We played without them letting me win, without any stupid awe towards me: they treated me as one of them. I felt great in those moments. Each point, no matter if I was winning or losing, was dear to me. I finally fitted in.

"If you want to, I can call a lady friend to keep you company tonight," one of Jewel's friend winked at me as we were going home.

"No, thank you," I said.

"Why not?" he was surprised, "you won't spend much money by your standard, and in that way you'd help her to maintain her family."

It's such a sad thing that, in the modern era, some people are still forced to do those kinds of things in order to survive. By that I don't mean only women selling their bodies to men, but also spending twelve hours behind a sewing machine, in inhumane conditions, breathing in different chemicals that were slowly killing them; all of this for just enough money to make it through the month.

Is there a possibility for everyone in the world to have enough money to buy food, sleep in warm beds, go to school and have the right to medical help? Through travelling, I realized that those things were quite enough to have a happy life. Still, in today's society, or at least in great part, there is one thing that moves everything – money. Whether you're hungry or not, healthy or sick, educated or not, it all depends on how much money you have.

However much you work hard or get by, that's how much of a good life you'll have – that is one of popular sayings of modern times. Has anyone wondered how much truth there is to that? If you're born in one of the slums of Bangladesh and as a nine-year-old you're forced to leave school to feed your family? If you're born into a family with many members because the more members you have, the more people who would need to work and bring money to the family.

Instead of the company of a prostitute, I accepted an invitation for a beer.

Even though alcohol was prohibited in Bangladesh, the rule wasn't applied to foreigners. Also, it wasn't applied to locals accompanied by foreigners. That was the reason why at least ten people joined us, even though there were supposed to be only four of us.

We found a restaurant in a side alley with a guard at the entrance that was illuminated only by candles on the inside in order not to attract too much attention; we ordered a drink for everyone. When I checked out the price list, which was identical to the one back home, and assumed that the bill would find its way to me, I informed them that I could only afford one round.

They didn't say a word, but started drinking foreign beers and some local spirits.

Not even fifteen minutes later they were all drunk.

I was sipping my beer slowly and observing the gathered crowd enjoying the forbidden fruit. I liked the fact that I could enable them to have a little fun, especially since they'd accepted me so readily in their group and offered me a place to stay. However, when the bill arrived, something changed within me.

The price of one round wasn't that expensive, but when I took into consideration the country I found myself in, well, then it definitely was. For a worker in a textile factory to be able to afford a night out like this one, they would have to work for at least ten days. For a prostitute in Bangladesh to be able to afford something like this, she would have to serve her clients for a whole week. The amount of money spent on those drinks would, most likely, suffice for many of the families I'd met in Kushtia for an entire month.

Those thoughts made me uncomfortable.

It wasn't okay, it wasn't fair, there was no need for a luxury of that kind, for showing off like that.

I missed Europe. I missed hitchhiking and sleeping on other people's couches, with a few Euros in my pocket. I would only spend the money on necessities and I didn't have to observe misery everywhere around me. The inhabitants of the countries I'd been in had perceived me as a poor person. And here, in Bangladesh, I was the sheriff.

I preferred the situations when I didn't have money. I liked me more. I took more care. I watched every Euro I spent and I was grateful for every extra piece of bread someone gave me.

"Shall we go?" I suggested to them, wanting to suppress the depressed thoughts.

We got up, divided ourselves in two groups and called two taxies. Six of us managed to fit in one taxi, and I was forced to share the co-driver's seat with Jewel, who sat on my lap. Some hundred metres later we were pulled over by the police.

"Excuse me, sir, but we have to do our job," a policeman with a big moustache apologized to me, while his colleagues frisked my friends and searched the trunk looking for a bottle of alcohol or something like that, "but, tell me, how do you like Bangladesh?"

Day 743.

I was in a luxurious neighbourhood of Dhaka, with four other pale-skinned ones and a driver who was always at our disposal. We had all been given the traditional clothes which we were supposed to wear to the different receptions and dinners during the following few days. Women wore colourful *saris*, while men wore *panjabi*.

Samai, just like the groom, came from a wealthy family, and the wedding reception was supposed to host more than thousand guests.

The first wedding day was dedicated to the bride. Her friends (luckily, I wasn't included) performed all sorts of shows and dances in her honour, so she could say goodbye to her maiden life. The initial ceremony was followed by a traditional ritual called *holud* in which people approached the bride and applied a natural cream made of saffron that was good for her complexion to her face, after which each person gave her a piece of food to wish her abundance of food in her new life.

The second day was dedicated to the groom, who went through the same procedure as Samai the day before. As the following day was the central ceremony of the wedding, after dinner we went to the bride's home and started with the preparations. While the father of the bride supervised the transformation of hundreds of sweet goats into a delicious meal, the female part of the company decorated their bodies with kana. They painted the bride's hands and feet hoping that the patterns would remain dark and visible even after the paint had been washed off. An old Bangladeshi belief said that the longer the stains remained dark, the greater the love between the bride and groom.

The house in which we stayed was enormous, and not less than seventeen members of the service, who'd been living there for generations, took care of it.

"They've played an important role in my growing up," Samai told me, introducing me to them and explaining that having servants was an old custom in Bangladesh, with both sides benefitting from it. On one hand, the house was clean, the meals were delicious, there was always someone to keep an eye on the children; while, on the other hand, the servants had a place to live, food to eat, and the possibility to go to school without the fear of losing their jobs. Talking to them I realized that, if I were ever to live in Bangladesh, I'd rather work in someone's service than in one of the factories I'd seen, or as a prostitute.

The next day started with both families coming together in the house of the bride where, after the imam's prayer and the consent of both sides, the couple was married. After a hearty meal we headed for the wedding hall where we were taken aback by the luxury, size and colour of the room, which was soon filled with more than a thousand people. More than 150 waiters had been hired for the job.

The bride and groom were dressed and decorated in gold and precious stones, which made the whole ceremony appear more like a royal wedding than a wedding of two of my peers.

Still, the peak of the evening was the moment when all the guests, dressed in expensive suits and silk saris, dug into the dishes in the traditional Bangladeshi way, with their bare hands.

I did the same thing, observing all the sparkle and comparing it to the misery I'd witnessed walking down the streets of the same city just as a couple of evenings before. The thoughts left me restless. I was lost between two extremes.

Leaving the hall, I smuggled out some of the food and gave it to a kid lurking outside, looking for someone to give him a few coins. He stuffed it all in his mouth, and I could discern 'thank you' in his bright eyes. I didn't see that brightness in the eyes of the guests who were in the wedding hall. No one, including me, had it. No one among us was hungry. We took the feast, the gold, the silk and the fireworks for granted.

That was the reason why, not wanting to wait until the end of the five-day ceremony, I packed my things in my backpack, went to the bus station and sat on the first bus heading east. It was time to return to reality and face hunger, thirst, and poverty, and to feel gratitude after satisfying those needs.

"May I sit next to you?" a polite teenager asked me in his impeccable English. He was carrying a transportable air-conditioner in his hands, taking care of it as if it was his most precious possession. Since I'd long given up on my fantasy of an uncovered beautiful Bangladeshi woman entering the bus, sitting next to me and looking for comfort after each sudden movement of the driver, I had no reason to turn him down.

"Thank you," the kid said politely, "my name is Sajid."

A couple of hours later, following good old Bangladeshi customs, I was having tea in Sajid's house in Comilla, in the company of his close and large family, and only two members of the family's staff.

"Unfortunately, I cannot invite you to stay at my house tonight," he said sadly during the dinner, "but some of my cousins are leaving tomorrow, so you could sleep at our place tomorrow."

I accepted the offer, as I did his suggestion that he be my guide and show me the interesting sights of Comilla. I went out on the street to look for a place to spend the night. It was dark, but there was still a glimpse of hope within me that I would be able to find a free place to stay so as not to break the only tradition I had kept alive on all of my journeys – not paying for accommodation.

I visited the local Catholic church, which was locked, hung around with some guys playing badminton in a park nearby, I even started making some arrangements with a guy to spend the night at his place, but at the last minute he changed the plan and took me to his friend who owned a hotel and who would give me a clean and cheap room where I could sleep.

I accepted that offer reluctantly, feeling the nostalgia. I missed Europe once again, its expensive hotels and CouchSurfers everywhere. In a country where I could afford a bus ride and sleeping in hotels, I didn't feel the need to test my limits. Consequently, there was no challenge, no adventure, no excitement.

I was lonely in the little hotel room. Perhaps for the first time since I'd been travelling. In Bangladesh I was either in the company of people who saw me as a movie star, a guru or a rich white man, or I was surrounded by the sparkle and luxury that looked so unnatural in that environment.

I went to an internet café in search of a word of comfort from my homeland far away: I was looking for anything that could put my mind at ease.

I found a message that had come to the CS site:

Hey Thomas,

We're two girls from Australia, travelling across Bangladesh. We've noticed that you're not far from us so if you're bored by travelling on your own and answering the same questions all over again by the dazzled locals, contact us, so we could answer the questions of the dazzled locals – together. We'll be in Srimangal in two days.

Hugs,

April and Taya

I must've have been a very good person in a past life.

Day 748.

A man with a big bowl in his hand was walking down the Comilla to Srimangal train, between the rows of shabby seats, saying out loud the name of the sweets he was selling. He tripped over someone's foot, and a fat sweet ball rolled out of the bowl and fell straight to the floor. He turned left, he turned right, picked it up, blew on it and returned it to the others.

And the best thing was that a person sitting next to me, who had probably seen the whole scene, called him over and bought one.

Oh, Bangladesh.

I had headphones in my ears and a book in my hand: I didn't want to talk to anyone until I reached my destination. I honestly didn't have the energy to make new friends, new acquaintances, superficial conversations that always led to the same thing, especially as the previous night I almost got myself married.

After I had spent the whole day sightseeing in the ruins of Buddhist temples with Sajid, and the afternoon in his house, we spent the evening at a neighbour's house, where we had dinner.

"Do you like Leza?" Sajid asked me when silence fell upon the room, winking at me as I explored my plate, filled with rice and a couple of pieces of chicken, with my right hand.

I felt Leza's eyes on me and the intense look her parents gave me as they waited for my answer; I blushed.

"It's not polite to talk during dinner." I managed to push the words through my mouth and started to fill it with food, chewing slowly so I could buy some time to come up with an answer.

I could've guessed that something like this would happen. When I entered their apartment, Leza was dressed in a colourful sari, much more festive than those that was usually worn for dinner, and she wore too much make-up. Her parents started complaining about her still being single, as she was already twenty-four. Too old for that country.

I somehow managed to change the subject after I'd licked my plate, but the kid couldn't be confused.

"Do you like Leza?" he repeated, louder than before.

While I was eating I was trying to come up with an answer that would be the most appropriate for the situation. I couldn't say 'yes' because: a) it wasn't true; and b) in their culture it would probably be understood as a half-arranged marriage. Still, I couldn't say 'no' either because: a) Leza would probably start crying, which would ruin the make-up; and b) it could be understood as an offense, after which her father might stab me with the sword hanging on the living room wall.

"I'll tell you when we get home," I replied to the little monster, smiling at him and at the others. No one assumed that the smile meant I'll beat Allah out of you when we get home.

"It would be wonderful if you married Leza," Sajid said as we returned home. "You could stay here so we could hang around every day."

Hearing those words I didn't want to kick his ass anymore. I still had to get used to the fact that in Bangladesh people grew quickly attached and that after you exchanged a few sentences they would start calling you brother.

"I love you, brother," Sajid whispered in my ear that night, sneaking into my bed and hugging me as I was pretending to be sleeping.

Srimangal, from the very moment I arrived at the train station, offered a different image than those I'd seen in Dhaka, Kushtia and Comilla. I even saw two white people on the streets. Merchants weren't marvels to me, but they invited me to their chambers, and every now and then a tourist guide would approach me offering his services.

I took a room in a modest hotel and welcomed the two girls with whom I'd be spending some time on the Road.

April and Taya had just turned nineteen and they had six months of volunteering in India and Nepal and a couple of months of wandering across nearby countries behind them. Their bodies were decorated with a couple of cool tattoos each, and they brought a small guitar with them. When April took it, hit A-minor and started playing a song by my favourite Australian band, I was overwhelmed by melancholy.

Hey little one,

I just wanted to let you know that I've run into two Australian girls who are just playing our song.

I hope India treats you well and that I'll see you soon, when you arrive in Europe, since we weren't able to meet in this part of the world.

Love, T.

Day 756.

"IIIIIIL!" I shouted, stopping by Lalon Shah's tomb, when I spotted my old friends, and the old man-prophet among them.

"IIIIIIL!" he replied, standing up and opening his arms in a hug.

After I visited the tea plantations in Srimangal, in the company of the two Australians, the green hills of Bandarban and the longest beach in the world at Cox's Bazar, I decided to spend the time I had until I went back home in the place where I had felt most at home – Kushtia.

This time, I only had one thing on my mind. This time I'd try to lose the royal treatment I'd had and live like my hosts, do the same things they did, see how it felt to be a local, and not a white tourist with a tourist's benefits. During my whole stay in Bangladesh I didn't manage to do it, except in some moments.

"Let's go to the river to wash our clothes," I said to Johnny, one of my faithful shadows, who knew a couple of words in English.

He took me to the place where a couple of weeks before I had had a ritual bath where there were a lot of women rubbing endlessly at a few colourful rags. He practically stole the clothes from my hands, grabbed the soap, found a big stone and started rubbing.

"Here, let me do the next one," I said when he was done with the first piece.

"Why, brother?" he said sadly, "why would you wash it, when I am here?"

He really didn't get it. From his perspective, he was the one who should be washing my dirty clothes, preparing something for me to eat, taking me wherever I wanted to go. Letting me do the dirty work was a direct punch to his pride.

"We'll make a documentary," I quickly came up with a reason to make it clear to him. "Here, take the camera, you'll shoot and I'll do the washing."

"I'll wash with you," he proposed a compromise. The camera ended up in John's hands, a guy I met that day, and who, as it turned out, had come from a city far away after a call from Boss, just because they knew I would be back in Kushtia.

So, Johnny and I washed the clothes on the river where baby Lalon was found floating in a basket. Many people gathered around to witness the unusual scene, but we managed to ignore them.

I thought about my parents, especially about my Mom, who often be-haved like Johnny and the others in Bangladesh. Why should I do some-thing when she could do it? How many times had she made my bed, with-out saying a word, cleaned the table after me, done the vacuuming when I didn't feel like doing it, picked up the dirty clothes scattered around the house, washed them, hung them to dry and later folded them and placed them in the wardrobe?

With the best intentions, and hoping that her son wouldn't have the hard life she'd had, with an immense quantity of love, she'd made a lazy, incapable man out of me. I let her do it for all those years. Why should I do something when she could do it?

I realized it the first time I'd moved out, when I realized the amount of work that was actually involved in keeping a small apartment clean and tidy and how much time it took to prepare lunch. And during those years she did all those things for me as well as having a proper job. For herself and for the three males living with her.

Above all, she tried to raise us properly in the best way she could.

From this perspective, as I was washing my clothes in a river in Bangla-desh, it seemed so unbelievable, so worthy of respect. I knew she would say to me something like: you're washin' your clothes in another part of the world, and if you were home you'd never think of doing it. And yet, she would be right. I couldn't explain it.

Maybe it was really necessary to change drastically your perspective to finally see certain things.

When we were done with the washing we headed to our building. As we were crossing the road I paid closer attention to many rickshaws that were constantly passing through our street.

"I would like to drive a rickshaw," I continued, expressing my wishes, but that time I was talking to my other shadow, Monir.

"No problem, brother," he replied, not even trying to talk me out of it.

Half an hour later he was back with a rickshaw, which he parked in front of the entrance to the building. I sat behind the handlebars and told him, just like I'd been told by many drivers who'd picked me up during my hitchhiking career: "Get in!"

After the first turn of the pedals I nearly managed to achieve the im-possible, which is turn over a three-wheel vehicle and scare Monir who wanted to get off the rickshaw, but couldn't out of fear (or maybe not to insult me). I continued driving slowly down the streets of Kushtia, dressed in a clean *lungi* and with a *gamcha* around my neck. If by doing that I was planning to become one of them, it rather backfired and instead my popularity kept on growing. For the first time in their lives, people watched in awe a white man driving a vehicle intended for the poorest; they commented loudly and some of them even gave me a spontaneous round of applause.

The pedalling itself wasn't as difficult as I'd imagined it when I was sitting behind locals who were much shorter than me down the city streets in Bangladesh. Still, I wondered how I'd have felt if I was of their build, driving a rickshaw with three people behind me, for ten hours a day for a low wage, as the locals do.

I was quite a lucky man, in fact, growing up in a wonderful country, surrounded by awesome people, never being hungry or bare-foot, being healthy, having a warm and safe place to sleep, free education, being able to do, basically, anything in the world for a living.

How ungrateful I was, in fact. How many times had I taken for granted all the beauty I'd been surrounded by my whole life, got mad at people who hadn't deserved it, wasted food, neglected my body, criticized my home, my neighbourhood, my city, my country, ditched school, whined when I had to pass exams at university?
That was the realization I was taking with me after I said goodbye to my friends, headed for Dhaka and got onto a plane that would take me back to my reality. It was the same realization I'd made during my first journeys across Europe and which was now confirmed: I was a spoilt brat, ungrateful and blind, ignorant of the awful global situation, especially in Third World countries.

It was the realization that I had to realize more things.

Day 794.

"Is your way of travelling dangerous?" Daniela wanted to know.

There we go. We finally arrived at that question. Pretty late, I must point out. Usually that was the first thing people asked me.

But why? Who had made them assume that this way of travelling was dangerous? That, after all, wasn't just a regular question. That was a question to which you could reply with an expected 'yes', or I could say 'no', which would be completely unexpected and surprising.

It was interesting to observe the eyes of the person you were talking to when you were answering that question. If you said 'yes', you could spot a small sparkle of relief in them, as if they were trying to say, I knew it, as if it was easier for them if they knew that along with all the beauty and the excitement of travelling there was also something less nice. And if, by any chance, you happen to say 'no' you could discern a tiny disappointment in them. Was it because they were sorry that they wouldn't be hearing a good story about you ending up behind the bars, being robbed or nearly raped; or was there any other reason? If there weren't any negative experiences they may end up wondering – why am I not travelling? They might think that all their fear was in vain. They might think that they'd been taught wrongly, that they'd been mistaken for their entire life.

Until you showed up and told them differently. You are the one to blame for realizing that they could've had the life they'd been dreaming of. You are the bad guy. Why had they even asked you anything in the first place? Their life was much prettier when they still thought that travelling, or at least in the way they could afford, was dangerous.

"No," I replied staring at Daniela's eyes.
"Well, do you watch TV, do you read papers? Do you know how dangerous it is to travel?" she responded in a goofy way.
I knew, right in that instance, that we were on the same page, just like when in a foreign country you could instantly recognize that a person spoke your language. I knew that, most likely, she'd travelled, too; she, most probably, had already had to face and fight prejudice, explain, justify...
"As a matter of fact, yesterday I listened to one song," I continued,

"there's a verse in which it says, 'they'll tell you about the sailing, those who've never raised an anchor.' Many people watch television, read newspapers, listen to horror stories. Based on my experience, after 17 thousand hitchhiked kilometres, with 200 different drivers, over 20 countries visited, more than 50 cities, all I can say is that I haven't had any negative experiences."

Numbers always worked. They were a good argument. They shushed those of little faith.

However, there was one. The one and only negative experience I'd had since I began travelling.

Day 420.

I got onto tram number 9 at the Borongaj roundabout in Zagreb.

The referee's final whistle had been heard fifteen minutes before and it marked the end of the biggest Croatian derby, that between Hajduk and Dinamo. It was a tie, 0:0. I knew it because I saw the score by accident on TV while I was hanging around in a friend's apartment with the guys from the university. My passion for Dinamo matches had left me long before that.

I was wearing jeans and a white sweatshirt. Tons of people got onto the tram, having just left Maksimir stadium. A couple of kids observed me closely and made some comment to themselves. I could sense the discomfort in the air. Probably because I was wearing white shirt, the colour of the opposing team.

"*Tovari, tovari!*"[23] a couple of people ran down the street, with baseball bats in their hands, shouting their lungs out, chasing a car with registration plates they didn't like.

"Open the door!" a few young supporters in the tram started shouting, rocking the tram, unable to hold on to get out of the tram and help their friends with the chase.

The driver opened the door as we were waiting for the green traffic lights, half of the tram rushed out and, still shouting, started running to catch up with the others.

How primitive, I thought to myself. And only a couple of months earlier I'd been one of them. I'd never chased the supporters of another club, I'd never thrown flares or got into a fight, but yes, I'd been one of them.

I glimpsed those guys who were still observing me closely. How great it would be if some shit happened, I thought. After hitchhiking through Serbia, Bulgaria, across Europe I could get into trouble in the centre of Zagreb, with the people with whom I'd recently shared the grandstands and a love of the club from Zagreb. How great would it be.

I got out at the main train station and entered a train heading south. I was only three stops away from my parents' house, situated in the suburbs of Zagreb. I found myself a compartment, sat next to an older woman, took out a book and started reading.

I heard someone walking with heavy steps and, a moment later, the

---

[23] A pejorative term for someone from Dalmatia.

door of the compartment was opened. Two guys in their twenties with an angry expression on their faces got in and started walking towards me.

"You stupid *Tovar*," they shouted while raising their feet and trying to hit me in the head, but expecting something like that, I managed to move back so they only brushed their sneakers against me and got my shirt dirty.

"Whaaa'?" I shouted, stepping back a bit further so that their sneakers wouldn't reach me on the second attempt.

They stopped with their legs in the air. Obviously they were confused by my dialect, which was definitely from Zagreb. They exchanged looks and dashed away.

The woman next to me started crying, the conductor came running to see what was going on, and I simply sat back into my seat with my whole body shaking.

Isn't this life funny? Really funny.

I heard a whistle from a guy with a red cap and the train slowly started moving southward.

Day 794.

The only negative experience I'd had since I began travelling happened in my birth town, at the main train station.

The conclusion was quite simple – there are idiots everywhere.

There are ways to protect yourself from them. For instance, you can stay at home, although home is a place where you can most easily come across them if you, let's say, turn on the TV and switch to the legislative session. And if you decided to leave your home there is always a chance that you will get into trouble. Now, will the trouble be in Africa or next to the traffic lights in front of your building? You can never tell.

The only thing you could tell for certain is that your life will end sooner or later. What matters is not when it will end, but what you'll be doing in the meantime.

"Where will you go next?" the interview was coming to an end.

"In a few days I'll be going to Portugal and then I'll be back in Zagreb to finally finish my studies."

That was the general plan.

"After that I'll be starting with my biggest journey so far," I took a deep breath, "and that journey will be called... Mom, cover your ears, *A Thousand Days of Summer.*"

There, I said it. That was the premiere of my next big project. My trip around the world. I could imagine my Mom lighting a cigarette, Dad getting up to grab a beer, one grandma starting to cry, the other one starting to pray the rosary, after milking the cow.

I could imagine my brother being proud of the kid he'd helped raise, my aunts calling me straight after the show and asking me whether I was being serious, my uncle wondering where had he gone wrong while teaching me the important life lessons, my friends concluding once again that I was crazy.

And Tanja, who would be pleased to hear that she was with me when I came up with that idea.

Day 775.

Are you home safe from Bangladesh? If you find someone to drop you off in Split, let me know.

Tanja

"I think I'm in love," I told to Tea and Maja, sipping my third beer.

"Yeeees?" they asked me, "who is she?"

"You know that video that is circulating online lately, *Last Year in 3 Minutes*?"

"Of course," Tea told me, "it's great."

"I know it is, I keep on watching it instead of studying for my final exam." I took a sip. "And another one in which she sings and plays guitar. Wow."

"And?" they asked me, "what are you going to do now?"

"I have no idea," I put the bottle on the table, "I am tempted to go to Split. I'm seriously considering that option. Especially now, when I have to study."

"I am going to Split tomorrow!" Maja shouted.

A coincidence?

I don't believe in coincidences.

Hey, Tanja!

You're busy this weekend and it would be a bad idea to come to see you, right? C'mon, make it easier for me by not leaving me any choice. Especially since I have an exam in a few days.

There were a couple of hours until midnight left, my last deadline to cancel my last exam – the same one I'd been postponing for years. So, instead of studying and getting it finally done, I was playing her videos for the thousandth time, both the first one and the second one. And thinking about how nice it would be to meet her.

I'm free as a bird this weekend. And I think that's an excellent idea.

Oh, well.

Well, nothing. See you tomorrow. I hope you have a couch available.

I cancelled my exam, put away my marketing book and went to bed. My heart was excited. Happy.

Day 776.

"Hi, Perko," I heard Maja's voice on the other line just as I was putting the last pieces of clothes in my backpack, "bad news. My trip's been postponed for some other time. Sorry."

I knew it sounded too easy.

I walked to the tollbooths going south, stuck out my thumb and slowly, in the company of a Russian truck driver, arrived at the toll booths in Split. Tanja got out of her mother's car and hugged me.

"Hi, Tom," she said, not taking the smile off of her face.

She was stunning. The immense positive energy that she radiated left the impression that no one could hurt her. At the same time, she was untouchable, and yet modest. A girl next door whose glass was always half full and who'd made a strong decision to enjoy life fully.

"Hi, Tanja," I replied and got into the car.

She told me straight away the thing that intrigued me the most – the story behind her video.

"Uh, don't ask," she said, tapping with her fingers the driving wheel following the rhythm of the song that was playing on the radio, "I had to do a presentation at my former university and the evening before the presentation was to take place I decided to make a presentation about the last year of my life, about quitting my job, about deciding to follow my dreams and starting a journey across Australia and South America."

"There isn't much to tell, really," she went on, "I uploaded it to YouTube simply so that I'd have it somewhere in case I lost my USB stick before the presentation, and a couple of days after that, people started sharing it on Facebook and I started receiving tons of messages...I mean, you of all people should know how these thing go."

"Yeah, I know," I said, "but, in my case, nothing has happened by accident. I upload everything online on purpose, so that people could see it."

"Why?"

"So that, for instance, you could send me a message to come to Split."

"*Touché*," she laughed, blushing slightly.

"But now the biggest challenge lies ahead of me," I sighed, "I have to finish university and find a way to earn a lot of money. Or go abroad and find a job there or come up with a project, a trip around the world maybe. I have to plan it all, come up with a story to connect it all, find sponsors, and leave."

"Have you come up with a story?"

"No. I have plenty of time until I pass my last exam, which I will have to take in the next exam session, in a few months, since I'm here now."

"I'm sorry."

"No, you're not."

"Oh, I know I'm not."

"Anyway, I'd like to leave Croatia and not come back so fast. I'd like to visit every continent, hitchhike, couchsurf, earn some money on the way, volunteer; you know how it goes."

"I know."

"So, as you already know how it goes, you could help me come up with a story."

"I could give it a try."

"That would be nice of you."

"Yup."

"Yup."

We entered her apartment, in fact her aunt's apartment, and opened the first can of beer. She went to the stereo, plugged in an mp3 player and started choosing the songs to play.

"Who do you listen to?" she asked.

"My parents," I replied, trying to be funny.

"Liar," she shouted, "'cause if you did, then you wouldn't be wanderin' around the world like you're doin' now."

"I see you have quite a lot of experience when you talk like that," I said.

"Uh. Imagine how my folks felt when, after a couple of years spent having an excellent job, reaching the position of the manager, I told them, listen, I'm off to travel the world."

"The same thing will happen to me, except that part with quitting the job."

"It appears that they don't care much about that. There are always other subjects to tackle: when you plan to settle down, what the others will say, when are you getting married, it's about time... You know how it goes."

"I know."

"And?"

"And what?"

"Who do you listen to?"

"Oh, right. Something with an acoustic guitar. Like your song on You-

Tube."

She didn't say anything. I didn't know whether it was because she blushed again or I reminded her of something I shouldn't have.

"I know," she finally said, "you'll love it."

I heard the familiar A minor from an acoustic guitar.

"I heard them when I was travelling across Australia," she explained, "and I loved them as soon..."

She stopped, noticing that there was something wrong.

"You don't like them?" she asked me from the hall.

"No, I love them," I laughed, "that's the problem. I'm afraid I'll love them for a long time."

"I sense there's a story behind that," she gave me an understanding look and sat next to me.

"You're smart."

We listened to the song, two people whose hearts and all of their body cells were touched by songs, mine by this one, hers by God-knows-which.

One kiss from you and I'm drunk up on your potion.
Big old smile is all you wore...

"So?" she asked as soon as the song was over, "who is she?"

"Who?" I was playing dumb.

"You know who." She wasn't that easily fooled.

She was so easy to talk to. We could finish each other's sentences and hear in them what the other one wanted to say, even though we said completely different things. She had a rare sense of humour, she knew how to laugh with others, but also to make fun of herself.

"Well," I started, taking another sip of the beer, "you know how it goes. Someone walks into your life, turns it upside down and walks out leaving the door open. And years after that you are still the victim of those feelings, no matter how many times you repeat that those feelings are better gone."

"And the victim of the songs that remind you of her," she added.

"Exactly."

"Why don't you visit her and close the door for yourself?"

"Well, that's the plan."

"When?"

"One day."

She got up and changed the music. Soon, she changed the subject, too.

We went out into the night in Split, had a couple of drinks and returned to the apartment. We relaxed on the couch and started watching a movie she'd been wanting to see for a while, *500 Days of Summer*.

"I like the title," I commented, not knowing that Summer was the name of the movie's protagonist. "It reminds me of a journey, as if someone was following the summer for five hundred days..."

"There's the idea for your trip," she hit me on the shoulder with her palm. "Either way, you'll do most of your travelling during the summer. As the seasons change, you'll change hemispheres. That's how I did it."

"It's a great idea," I said, "but, five hundred days seems too little. What do you say about one thousands days?"

"A thousand days of summer," she said solemnly, "it sounds great."

"A thousand days of summer," I repeated, "it really does."

We exchanged looks full of pride high-fiving each other at the same time. We were a great team.

The male protagonist of the movie, Tom(!), who is convinced that the whole point of one's life was to meet Miss Right, falls head over heels in love with Summer. His life finally makes sense, everything works for him, birds are chirping, and stuff like that. Summer, on the other hand, is a cold beauty who claims from the very beginning that she doesn't believe in love and that she doesn't want a boyfriend. She doesn't feel at ease being someone's girlfriend. Of course, the two of them hook up and after a while it's all downhill for them...

Where had I heard that story before?

"Tom, Tom," Tanja was waking me up since I'd fallen asleep at the very end of the movie.

"What?" I muttered, not opening my eyes.

"Go to bed, the couch is uncomfortable."

Day 794.

"A thousand days of summer?" Daniela asked.

"Yes," I confirmed, "hitchhiking around the world, starting this summer, basically with no money, earning some money on my way..."

The initial idea was to start the journey with a thousand Euros and travel until I don't have any money left. Once I'm left without any money, I'll try to get by in any way possible. I was secretly hoping that another thing would work out – that MasterCard would prolong their sponsorship, even after Bangladesh and Portugal, and sponsor my biggest, longest and most interesting journey.

"Good luck," she said as she was signing off, "we'll try to keep our show running so that when you come back to Croatia, we will host you again in the show."

"Fine by me."

"Tomislav, thank you a lot."

More applause, after which I walked off the stage.

"A thousand days, ha?" Shale asked me immediately after the interview, "you could get a bit bored."

"Well, fuck," I said, "I need to travel all the continents and the cheapest way to do it is – not going back home."

I met with Tanja who was spending a lot of time in Zagreb lately. She was counting down her last days in Croatia. She was waiting for a work permit from the British embassy so she could book a flight to London and move there. That had been her wish from when she was little.

Our relationship was wonderfully relaxed since we knew that, soon, we'd have to part: her path was leading her to London, while my path would lead me around the world, as soon as I passed my last exam. Our conversations were usually about happy subjects because we didn't see any point in sad ones.

"Hello," she responded to her mobile phone. We were headed for the bus station from where she would go to Split that evening and then proceed to London. This was the call she'd been expecting. The call that would confirm that her visa was ready and that she should start packing straight away and move to another part of Europe. The call that would, inevitably, bring with it the moment when we'd have to say goodbye to each other.

However, by the tone of her voice, I noticed that there was something wrong.

"Well?" I asked when she hung up.

"Oh, don't ask," she replied with a sad voice, possibly the saddest I'd ever heard from her, "the employers have screwed something up with the application so I'll have to wait for another two or three months."

"Oh," I said, "what are you going to do now?"

"I don't know," she continued with the same tone, "it's been like this for months: I live in Split at my parents' place, waiting for the stupid visa so I can open a new chapter in my life; I do nothing except wait, wait and wait. And now I'll have to wait some more. I feel like forgetting all about it and moving somewhere else."

I got an idea.

"Come to Portugal with me," I said without much thinking.

"What?" her tone of voice was a bit different, "where has this come from?"

"There, it just came to my mind," I smiled, "you've said yourself that you have nothing to do, and I could use the company."

"You know that I don't have any money."

"MasterCard will pay for everything," I said, "we can arrange everything: you can be the official photographer and camera woman, and instead of being paid for doing it, they could cover your travel expenses. It's a win win situation."

She stood in front of me and looked me straight into the eyes, checking how sure I was of my decision.

"Oh, Tom," she threw herself into my arms.

Day 855.

I left the building of the Faculty of Economics, sat on the bench in front of it and started crying.

After eight years spent at that faculty, I'd finally passed my last exam. I'd finally got such a heavy burden off my chest that I couldn't do anything other than let it all out and cry.

"Colleague, congratulations," my professor from marketing offered me her hand, after signing my index and giving me a B, "I wish you all the luck on your next journeys."

"Thank you," I was too excited, "but, how do you know...?"

"Do you think that someone else corrects my exams?"

She simply smiled and gave me back the index.

"Send a postcard every now and then."

I remembered instantly what I'd written at the end of the exam:

Dear Professor,

Maybe the theory of marketing isn't my strongest point, but I've had quite a success in the practical part lately. A year ago I started writing about my journeys and promoting myself on the Internet, in the media, and especially on social networks. And I didn't have to spend anything on it, so I applied the theory you've taught me.

As a result, I've appeared on television a couple of times, in the newspapers, on different Internet portals, and I have more than five thousand followers on Facebook.

If the theory won't suffice for a D, I hope that, at least, the practice will.

Since I got a B, I guess the theory was good, too.

I called my Mom, and Tanja too. I wanted to thank her for forcing me to finally study hard for the exam.

She was wonderful. The three weeks we'd spent together in Portugal had convinced me that we were an excellent couple, we didn't have a single argument, we always had something to talk about, she hitchhiked and couchsurfed without complaining about it, she drank with me on benches, ate food bought in supermarkets, cooked – she was everything I was looking for.

There was only one thing that bothered me every once in a while: an Australian song that kept on playing in my head, even though it was supposed to end two years ago.

I tried to console myself that, maybe, I needed a bit more time. And when I was with Tanja, time seemed to fly by faster and less painfully.

I went home and typed a sentence.

What do you say about joining me on my trip around the world?

I checked the sentence once again and pressed ENTER. Not even half an hour later, my phone rang.

"My cake's just burnt because of you and your e-mail," she said, "frankly, no one has ever offered me anything more beautiful."

She fell silent. I knew the meaning of the silence.

"But?" I asked.

"You know how long I've been waiting for London," she finally said, "and you know how much I'm looking forward to it. Now it's finally here, only a couple of weeks away, and I really don't know if I could give up on it and join you."

"And you know how much I wanted to do it," she added after a few moments of silence, "if it'd happened earlier or if you could start with the journey later..."

I understood her completely. When I thought about it, I couldn't have expected a different answer. She had her dreams, and now I was asking her to give up on them and go on a journey with an unknown man whom she'd met only a few months before. Only a crazy person would do that.

I would also refuse to follow someone else's dreams.

"Still, you can come to London with me," she suggested at the end. "At least until you start your adventure."

Actually, maybe I could.

Day 942.

Chloe

I punched the pillow on my clean and fresh-smelling bed in the London hotel room where I'd spent the past few weeks planning the details of my upcoming journey, choosing the route and promoting my Facebook page. Tanja was in her office, a few blocks away.

I should have punched myself and not the innocent pillow. Or maybe even my stupid feelings, which woke up as soon as I saw who the e-mail was from and grew even stronger when I read the content.

Was she ever going to leave me alone?

There was only one way to find out.

I'll be in Zagreb in a couple of weeks and I'll be staying there for a month before I go on my journey. You know where you can find me.

T.

I wanted to see her in order to have closure on our story once and for all. I wanted to make sure that during those past years I'd been in love with an imaginary person with whom I'd spent only a few days in Zagreb. The person who was the reason I turned my world upside down and faced the Road. The person who used my heart and took off forgetting to put it back where it belonged. The person who contacted me two years later saying that she wanted to see me.

Day 219.

"Come," she told me as we were taking a stroll down the street in the centre of Zagreb and exploring the Solar system, one of the mysteries of my city that I often explain to the tourists, "take a look at those two girls sitting at that table."

She pointed to two attractive girls who were sipping a juice through straws, all dressed up for a Sunday walk in the city. Each of them was looking in the opposite direction. They had serious expressions on their faces, they showed a total lack of interest in everything, they seemed to be lifeless, lost with their thoughts wandering around. They were gorgeous, and still – empty on the inside.

"And now, take a look at those two," she pointed to another table.

At the other table were also two girls, average looking, not wearing any make-up, wearing plain clothes. They were in a world of their own, talking excitedly to each other and laughing carelessly. They didn't pay attention to the people around them or the opinions these might have about them. They were glowing.

"Isn't that nice?" she asked me, all radiant. She didn't wait for an answer, but she simply walked down the street, in her summer dress, not looking back.

I stood there, watching her and wondering how it was possible that, after she looked at me with her blue eyes on my doorstep, everything else became so irrelevant...

When I was with her, time flew by irregularly, following rules of its own. The space surrounding us was foggy and blurry, the sounds were muffled; I felt alive, awake, invincible. And when she'd give me one of her looks, my feeling of being alive would instantly be covered by a feeling of helplessness. I was naked in front of those eyes. I knew that, if she kept her eyes on mine long enough, she would recognize panic, fear and longing. At the same time, I couldn't take my eyes off of her bright face, loose hair, colourful dress and bare feet.

She was a few years younger than me, but as far as the spirit was concerned, you could say she was much older. She'd left her home when she was eighteen and started making her way in this world. She'd lived on three different continents, was fluent in three languages, did all kinds of jobs to be able to afford food, had been through different kinds of life challenges trusting only herself. She'd travelled, hitchhiked, slept in parks and on train stations, but she'd always been careless and playful like a child.

She was good at noticing details and everyday magic as she was conscious that they might not be there tomorrow. She drew, made sculptures, picked up trash from the street and threw it in the rubbish bin, preached about the importance of taking care of the environment; she was always ready to discuss the arguments for being veg(etari)an, to discuss the political bullshit we were fed with every day, and was never afraid to state her opinion loud and clear.

I was done. Head over heels in love.

I wanted to have that passion with which she lived her life. I wanted to have her.

Still, I didn't dare to take the first step, tell her anything, go for all or nothing. I felt that I wasn't good enough for her. What did I have to offer her? To a girl who'd been everywhere around the world, who was so experienced, who had a clear opinion about everything that mattered to her. To a girl who could disarm any man with her smile, who could spend the whole night discussing subjects about which I was completely clueless.

"You're late for work," she whispered in my ear as she sneaked into my bed on her last day in Zagreb.

Her soft voice and the warmth of her body worked as an instant wake-up call. I took a deep breath, inhaling the arousing scent of her skin. My heart was beating heavily in my chest, but I still didn't want to open my eyes, afraid that the moment would be soon over.

"I don't care," I finally said, "it's nice here."

I put my arms around her waist and finally opened my eyes. I let her see in them everything I'd been hiding from her for the past few days. Fear, love, lust. She could have them and do with them whatever she pleased. Either way, she'd be gone soon.

She observed them for an eternity. She saw everything that there was to see and finally, with her eyes wide open, she got very close, gently placing her lips on mine.

In that moment I could die happy.

"And?" she asked abruptly interrupting the most beautiful kiss, placing her head on my chest. "Now what?"

"Why are you asking me that?" I asked calmly, although I was anything but calm, "you kissed me. What do you want?"

"I don't know," she replied mischievously. You could never tell if she was playing with you or whether she was being serious. "However, I do know that I like you."

That was enough for me. Nothing else mattered. I wanted to see her again and feel what I'd been feeling for the past few days. I wanted to kiss her again and have a re-run of the fireworks I felt then. But I wasn't sure if that would be possible, being already acquainted with the destiny of travellers – the ones who always leave. They would always leave, no matter how much chaos they left behind.

"Let's meet again," I suggested, after we shared a couple of moments of tenderness. I was completely ready to go after her, wherever she wanted to go, live off of air and her presence, even though I knew, from my own experience, that obsession wasn't a good start for anything. I couldn't help myself. I was definitely obsessed.

"But, how?" she asked sadly, "I'm returning to Berlin today, and in a few months I'll be off to Australia, and you're staying here to finish university, find a job, repay the debt... Our lives are going in different directions."

"Frankly, I have no idea how," I wasn't giving up. "I could pay you a visit in Berlin before you go. It's not that far away."

Australia also didn't seem that far away at that moment, only if she felt what I felt.

"You know everything," I told her that afternoon, on one of the platforms of the main train station, "you know how I feel about you and that I would want to be next to you, anywhere, even for a short period of time, under any condition."

"I know," her answer was short, observing me.

"When you return to Berlin, think about everything," I continued, "if you want me to join you there so we could spend some time together, let me know."

She gave me a strong hug, and I hugged her even more strongly. In case I wouldn't have another chance.

Day 271.

"Bro!" Filip called me as we were arriving at a gas station somewhere in Slovenia, "remember: minimal risk."

"No worries," I said, taking my backpack from the trunk, "just take care that Mom doesn't find out I'm hitchhiking. Oh, and if you happen to see *Into The Wild* running on television, don't let her watch it."

He left, leaving his brother to the mercy of the Road, and it wasn't easy for him to do it. He didn't speak much as we were driving to Slovenia, and as he was leaving I noticed his right palm passing over his face.

In the past twenty days, since she sent me the e-mail that she was expecting me in Berlin, I quickly rearranged some things in my life. I did it in the only way I could – to the extreme. In a short time period I had so many things to do. A situation like that called for extreme actions.

I knew that I wanted to go to Berlin and spend some time with her. I didn't know how long it would last. But I knew what was keeping me from doing it.

"We need to talk," I said to Martina and Mongoose as we stood on the same terrace as a couple of months earlier when I started with the first drastic change in my life. Now it seemed to me that that was another life. I loved those two, I loved the bar, I loved the customers I'd served every day, I loved the places we went to after closing the bar.

"There isn't an easy way to say this," I started talking with a tickle in my throat, staring at the floor, "I cannot work here anymore."

They became serious; Martina grabbed a pack of cigarettes and lit one.

"Have we done anything?" she asked, shaken up a bit.

"You know you haven't," I replied quickly, "you know I love you like a brother and sister; you know that I adore this place, but I have to leave this city, I have to find peace. I really have to."

Mongoose looked at me as if he'd assumed something like that would happen. He was sad when he heard the news, but he wasn't surprised.

"Chloe?" he asked.

"Chloe," I answered.

We got wasted that night like never before. We had to celebrate the new beginning, instead of crying about the end.

Since I'd lost my job, it was obvious that I wouldn't have any money to pay the rent and the bills. I told that to my roommate the next day.

He was really a dream roommate. We'd never had a single argument, let alone a fight, during those three years we lived together. We knew when it was someone's turn to cook or clean and we knew when to leave the place when the other one was bringing a date. We were born less than 24 hours apart and, in many things, we were like brothers.

"Chloe?" he asked.

"Chloe," I answered.

I moved my things to my parents' house, informed them that I would be travelling to Berlin by train to visit a girl, promised to call them every day, put my backpack on for the fourth time and sat in my brother's car for the lift to Slovenia.

I had three hundred Euros in my pocket and a couple of months left until the next exam session. There wasn't a single word that could describe the excitement I felt. I was going on the road, no return date, to visit a girl I hadn't stopped thinking about since I met her. And I had met her fifty-four days before that.

Not that I was counting.

Two hundred and fifty kilometres, 3 rides and 5 hours later I was in Vienna. I survived my first travelling encounter with the police. Near Graz they stopped me, but instead of giving me a ticket for walking along the highway, they simply gave me a lift to the next gas station, and an apple and a sandwich. Nice people, even though they were cops.

"How come, of all the cities in the world, you've ended up in Vienna?" I asked Zuli, my CS host, as we were sipping a beer in a famous bar in Vienna. The price was also famous – 3.60 Euros. When I paid for a round I started looking closer at the money I was spending. One beer was, in fact, one per cent of my budget. Two beers, two per cent. I could afford a trip around Europe, as long as my budget didn't go over one hundred beers in that bar.

I had a new unit of measurement.

"One day I took a map of Europe, closed my eyes and said to myself, wherever my finger lands, I'll go there," she said, with her eyes closed, pointing to an imaginary map. "My finger landed on Austria, where I've been living for a couple of years now. I'm studying and working. It's nice."

I didn't know by what I was enchanted more: by her story, her way of telling it, or her. Most probably, by everything.

From the very beginning, the story was more than unbelievable. The very fact that a person could let herself go to a coincidence, destiny, call it as you will, and start a new life, in another part of the world, with no one around, not knowing the language, arriving there for the first time. How much courage does it take to do it? How much faith?

Above all, Zuli was probably the sweetest creature I'd ever met. She had dark and Latin American complexion, long dark hair, brown eyes hidden under slightly hooded eyelids with an honest, shy and seductive smile. She was so beautiful that only after the second round of beer, when I went to the bathroom and faced that well-known half-drunk expression in the mirror above the sink, I had to remind myself why I had come to Vienna.

"This morning you headed for Berlin, to meet a blonde Australian girl," I said irritated, regarding the happy man in the mirror, "you fool."

"So what?" the reflexion answered.

"So what?" I was pissed. "You've mixed up your life, left everything behind and gone to see her. And on your first day, that is on your first night, you're out with a gorgeous girl and all you're thinking about is how nice it would be to kiss her soft lips. Where would that lead?"

"I have no idea and I don't care," he carried on, "I'm tired of thinking too much about the future, making theories, plans... I mean, you have no idea what will happen in Berlin. I hope you realize that. If not..."

"If not what?" – I asked.

"You know the reaction of a heart when expectations aren't realized," he reminded me, "so, enjoy the moment, don't expect anything, be honest and try your best not to hurt anyone."

"What do you know?" I turned around and returned to the table.

We had another *Weißer Spritzer* and went to her apartment where, like a true CouchSurfer, I fell asleep on the couch, innocently and with the blond Australian girl in my thoughts.

Day 277.

I spent three nights in Prague and two in Dresden, and finally, on my sixth day of travelling I arrived in Berlin. The final destination.

On my way to Berlin I had one of my most memorable hitchhiking experiences. In Dresden I met with Josh, a friend I'd met in Prague and had hosted a few months before in Zagreb. We met in the centre and headed for a gas station to start hitchhiking.

We walked carelessly by the road looking for a good place to start hitchhiking. Suddenly, we heard the squeal of tires and a VW Golf pulled over next to us. Two dubious guys got out, wearing jeans and sweatshirts, with caps on their head. Both of them had pierced noses and eye-brows. They started walking towards us, with their arms wide open.

"Free hugs?" one of them asked, stepping closer.

And then it hit me. I burst into laughter. There was still a FREE HUGS sign on my backpack from Prague, the guys saw it, had a spontaneous reaction and got out of the car to have a hug.

"Where are you headed?" the other one asked, after a real man hug.

"Berlin," we said, still smiling. We knew what was coming next.

"So are we!" our new friends exclaimed, "get in."

Oh, the universe.

As we were approaching Berlin, my heart started growing restless.

"Nächster Halt[24]: Eberswalder," the woman on the PA system announced.

I walked out of the U-bahn, turned right and found what I was looking for: Schonhauser Allee, number 146.

The address Chloe had given me.

I climbed up the stairs; there were so many of them. Third floor, no elevator. My palms were sweaty, I felt butterflies in my stomach, heart beating heavily like never before, and my legs never felt heavier. It seemed like an eternity before I came to her door and pressed the bell.

I heard steps from within.

I took a deep breath.

The door opened and a guy stood in front of me.

I exhaled.

---

[24] Next station.

"Hi," I greeted him feeling a bit disappointed, "is Chloe maybe here?"

"Chloe?" he was confused, "I don't know any Chloe."

"Chloe?" a new face appeared behind the door, "she went outside with some other guys to buy groceries, she should be back soon. Come in, you can wait for her inside."

I entered an apartment that was, basically, a squat. At least ten people lived there, there were all kinds of instructions and rules stuck on the walls, the groceries in the fridge were marked in different colours, depending on whose was what, there was a list of house chores, and so on. I realized that my old apartment didn't come even close to a squat, there were no rules, the tenants knew each other and the fridge was always empty.

My guide offered me a tea. He was explaining to me how things functioned in the apartment when I heard steps coming from the outside, the rattle of keys and the sound of someone unlocking the door.

Impolitely I turned around just as my guide was in the middle of his monologue and looked at the kitchen door. I heard a dialogue in German, which I didn't understand. Footsteps. And then, through the open door, I saw loose blonde hair. And she saw me. Time stopped, just like my heart.

The little blonde girl pointed her finger to me and yelled, "you!"

We approached each other and hugged.

"I totally forgot you were coming today," was the first thing she said after a long and warm hug. Her voice was exactly the same as I remembered it: innocent, child-like and playful. Still, there was something different about her eyes.

"I totally forgot you were coming today," she repeated, interrupting our eye contact and leaving my arms to the mercy of gravity. She noticed I'd heard her even the first time, but I wasn't listening. I studied the tone of her voice and the warmth of her eyes. Or maybe even the coolness as I finally understood what she'd just told me. Suddenly, my entire body went cold.

She totally forgot the fact that I was coming. While I had spent months waiting for that moment.

No, she couldn't have forgotten. We'd exchanged an e-mail the day before saying that we'd be seeing each other the following night. She was a smart girl so I knew she wouldn't forget that easily. No, there was something else involved. Whatever it was, it wasn't good.

"Get yourself ready," my reflection in the mirror, which I managed to catch, winked at me, "and don't say I didn't warn you."

I was ready. It was extremely difficult observing her losing herself in the words she exchanged with me; observing her do different chores around the place, laughing forcedly at her roommates' jokes. My presence made her nervous. But not nervous in the same way she made me. She didn't want to be next to me. She didn't enjoy my presence. She wasn't completely present.

And I didn't know why.

"Shall we take a walk?" I asked when I realized that we wouldn't be able to have a normal conversation in the noisy crowded apartment.

"Sure," she accepted and turned to the others. "We are taking a walk, does anyone want to join us?"

Her roommates became quieter and refused politely. It seemed that they knew, just as I did, that they had nothing to do with us. She was the only one not to understand it.

"I'm glad no one wanted to join us," I said as we were out on the street, "I've come to Berlin to spend some time with you, to talk to you, not with your roommates."

She didn't say anything.

"Still, I see I'm the only one wanting to talk," I stood in the middle of the street and took her by hand.

"Look. There is only one thing I need from you. Only one. Honesty. Quick, painful, whatever. I think I've deserved it, even if we disregard the fact I've travelled half of Europe only to see you."

She lowered her eyes, let go of my hand and continued walking.

"I've told my best friend about you," she said after a while, "I've told him about Tomislav whom I met in Zagreb and whom I liked very much. *Thomas Love*, he commented. It made sense. I liked the way he called you that. Thomas Love. It sounded almost identical to your real name. And it fits perfectly into our story and the things you'd made me feel."

"But?" I asked her. You could always sense when a but was coming.

"But," she stopped, "we're not on the same page in life. I'll be soon going home, after a few years of travelling. I'm fully concentrated on that. And I really wouldn't like to start something that will be over soon."

"How do you know it will be over?" I was slowly realizing that the ship had started to sink and that there was nothing I could do about it.

"I just know," she continued. "I really like you. I find you attractive. I like you being next to me. And you'll always be 'mine'. Still, at this moment, I cannot give you what you want from me. The thing that you've come here for. The thing you think you deserve. I'm not ready for it."

"Why are you thinking about it so much?" I was angry. "All that matters is this moment and what we have now. How can we know what the tomorrow will bring? Can't we simply enjoy each other while it lasts, while we're here?"

"I can't." She looked at the ground. "Try to understand me. I've been through similar situations in the past and they never turned out well. The only thing that remained were the scars."

"But this isn't the past, we're in present." I wasn't giving up.

"Why would you even want to be with me?" she gave me a sad but firm look, "you don't know me."

I looked her straight in those eyes, trying to reach as deep I could. I couldn't possibly know what she was fighting with. All that I knew was that she was trying really hard to push me away from her.

"Because I love you, Chloe," I managed to mutter.

"I'm sorry, but I don't love you," she told me briskly, quickly and firmly. No hesitation.

That was the moment. The ship had sunk. Silently, no sound from a single crew member, no attempts to save themselves.

It was as if it had never even sailed.

I kissed her and gave her a strong hug. Her body was cold and lifeless. Her eyes were empty. Just like the eyes of those two gorgeous girls she'd noticed that day on the street in Zagreb. The spark I could see in her eyes during those days was gone.

Day 962.

"So, Tanja, what are we going to do?" I started an unavoidable conversation during our last dinner together, the conversation we'd been successfully avoiding. After two months of tenderness, endless conversations, walks in the rain, endless laughs and huge amounts of ice-cream, I was leaving London and going to Zagreb to start my trip around the world.

"I've given it a lot of thought," she began, obviously well prepared. "No matter how much I wanted to go with you, I owe it to London and to myself to stay here and see how things will work out. If I leave before even giving it a try, I will always ask myself that one question - what if. And you wouldn't want a girl like that as a company on your trip around the world."

"Still, if you stay, you'll always be asking yourself how it would be if you had gone with me," I added.

"You're right," she said, "and that's why I'll be visiting you every now and then. Just to check are you doing OK."

I laughed, even though I didn't feel like laughing.

"And on your five hundredth day of travelling, in the middle of your journey, I'll leave my job, London, everything...and join you," she said happily, trying to cheer me up.

"I don't know if I could do that," I said quietly, "you know the reason why I'm starting this journey. I want to try out something new, leave my old surroundings, I want to discover my passion, my interests, my attitudes. Discover myself. And I'm not really sure that I'll able to do it if I leave something behind. I'm not sure that I'll be able to survive waiting possibly for a year, or a year and a half."

She wasn't happy anymore.

"Freedom," I said after a while, "that's what I'm looking for. If I go, and leave a girl in London behind me, a girl who will be thinking about me, to whom I'll have to write and who I'll have to call telling her how nice it would be if she could be with me, I won't be free as I'm hoping to be. I will also need a free heart, or a person who holds my heart right next to me. We've talked about long-distance relationships and we've agreed that they never work out."

"But we've never talked about us!" she exclaimed. "How could we have known that we would become the thing we have become? I thought we were stronger than this. Who cares about the kilometres that will separate us?"

"I do," I said, almost inaudibly.

"What do you want?" she asked, with a voice in which I could sense infinite sadness. "Do you want us to break up?"

"I don't know what I want," I quickly said.

Although I knew.

I wanted to leave London as a free man. I wanted to leave Croatia, move east, as a free man. I wanted to wander around the world on my own, free. I didn't want to leave people behind me who would be waiting for my return, who would want me to call them wherever I went, who would be worried about me wherever I went.

My family was more than enough.

And I couldn't tell her what I wanted. Her, a person who was probably the best, the sweetest and the happiest I'd ever known in my whole life. I couldn't make her feel so sad, I couldn't hurt her.

I couldn't, although I sensed that I would have to do it.

"We'll see how it will work out," I tried to give her the most sincere smile I could at that moment. Still, I was a coward.

She didn't know it. She didn't see it. She wouldn't let herself see it. Or I didn't try hard enough for her to see it.

Day 1000.

Hey little one,

It seems that you won't be visiting me in Zagreb. But it's okay. I don't hold any grudges against you.

In less than 24 hours I'll be starting my long awaited Journey. On the same day, just two years after I was off to Berlin to visit you. In the end, that turned out to be my first big journey.

Now I'm here, just about to head off. And it all makes sense now. It feels right.

All I wanted to say to you is – thank you. Thank you for being you and for everything you've done for me. And if it happens that I never see you again, you know everything. Or at least you should know.

Be happy, Chloe.

I closed my laptop and put it in my backpack, along with the things I'd need during the following one thousand days of Life on the Road. A tent, an inflatable mattress and a sleeping bag. A few pieces of summer clothing. A raincoat. My laptop, mobile phone, camera, all kinds of chargers, batteries, external hard drives. A toiletry bag. First aid kit. A torch and a Swiss knife. My stuffed sheep.

I put my guitar over one shoulder and left home. I took another look at my backyard, my balcony, Mom's most scented rose in the garden. I got onto a train and went downtown. I had some things to do before I left.

"Mister Perko," a nice lady invited me to approach the counter at the Indian embassy, "the consul would like to have a word with you."

"No problem," I replied and followed her into an airy and spacey office where a man with a smile on his face was waiting for me, a man who had the power to make my life a misery.

"Sit down, please," he asked me, pointing to the comfortable armchair, "I've noticed that in your application for a tourist visa you didn't attach a return plane ticket."

"That's right," I replied casually, with a smile on my face, "my plan is to get to India by land."

"By land?" he was surprised, "do you know that you will have to pass through some very dangerous areas?"

"I'm well aware of that," I was self-assured, or at least I sounded as though I was, "I already have visas for Pakistan and Iran in my passport."

"Hmmm," he checked the fresh stamps in my passport. "What do you do, mister Perko?"

"I have a degree in economics," I replied proudly, "more precisely, in tourism. And basically, my journey can be seen as a practical part of my studies, having listened to the theory for so many years."

He laughed and browsed through a bunch of papers and my passport once again.

"No problem, could you wait in the lobby," he finally asked, "and, please, take care of yourself."

"Thank you a lot," I said, relieved, "I will."

I left the embassy and went to Iva's office.

"Good news," she was waiting for me at the door, "MasterCard agreed to sponsor your trip around the world. They agreed to all of your terms."

"To all the terms?" I repeated.

"All of them," she winked at me.

Unbelievable.

That was the moment I had been hoping for all those years. The moment I got a dream job: I'd travel around the world, enjoy, take photos, write about it and be paid for it very well. Extremely well, indeed. It was a well-paid job that, if I didn't spend any of the sponsor money and respected the contract to the end, would give me the exact amount of money I needed to repay the five-figure debt that was constantly on my mind and which had been giving me nightmares for all those years.

It seemed surreal. I felt as if I was watching a bad Hollywood movie, or reading an equally bad book in which the protagonist, after finding himself in a desperate situation at the beginning and after facing numerous obstacles, finally gets what he wants, although he didn't know what that was.

A happy ending which was, in fact, only the beginning.

The movie will definitely have a sequel.

"Hi, Mom," I called her to communicate the good news, "the people from MasterCard agreed to be my sponsors."

"Bravo," she replied sadly. After all, it was the last day she'd be spending with her son for the following God-knows how many months.

"See, everything has turned out well," I told her, reminding her of a hug I'd given her before going to Spain and of my promise that one day, everything would make more sense, "I'll get paid enough money to repay all my debts."

"If you stay here, your father and I will return all that money," she said, "just don't go."

My heart stopped beating for a second. I knew she really meant it. I knew she was ready to do anything, even the most desperate measures, to stop her son from going away.

"I have to do it, Mom," I barely managed to say, "you know I have to."

She knew it. She knew me too well not to know it.

"See you tonight," I said and hung up the phone.

"So, you're really going away?" Nina asked me over a beer.

"So, I'm really going away," I replied, slowly starting to realize that this was really it. I only had to say goodbye to my friends and family, spend the night at my brother's place and my Journey could start.

"Everything all set up?" she gave me a look that reminded me of the one she'd given me before my first trip alone to Amsterdam: if it wasn't for her, I probably wouldn't have done it.

"All set up," I replied, "Just..."

"Just?" she repeated.

"During all those months, ever since I got the idea of travelling the world, I've been looking for a mission. Some aim for the journey, a motto. And I'm not sure that I've managed to find it."

"Why do you need a mission?" she wanted to know, "you travel for yourself, not for others."

"You could say that," I agreed. "I don't know, I'd like to have some sort of a story. The closest I've come was the promotion of alternative travelling styles, hitchhiking, CouchSurfing, volunteering and stuff like that, proving to people that you could travel almost for free.

"And that isn't enough?"

"I don't know... I wanted something better, something more inspiring."

"And what about your sheep?" she asked.

"What about her?" I was surprised. Maria Juana was the only thing in my backpack that didn't have any practical use. She'd been with me on all of my journeys, from my first wanderings across Europe up until now. We made a good team.

"She could be your story," she suggested, "take photos of her all around the world: she could represent your life path, she could tell your story. She ran away from her herd, with a smile on her face, looking for things that make her happy and what fulfils her. Just like you."

So simple, practical and true.

We finished our beer and moved to the bar where I would have my goodbye party.

We had a few rounds of drinks, my parents, close family and a couple of my closest friends arrived, and also a few people I had never seen before. The atmosphere was high. I was celebrating a new beginning, not crying over the end of something.

Until the moment I feared the most.

"We're going home," Mom and Dad said, standing up. I followed them with heavy legs, the same as that day on the staircase in Berlin. I walked them to the entrance and stopped.

"Everything is going to be okay," I put a smile on my face and hugged them. First my Dad.

He hugged me and started sobbing. The strongest man I knew was falling apart in my arms. I was falling apart, also. I stepped back, trying to hide the tears, and hugged my Mom. She was crying, too.

"Don't worry, Mom," I was sobbing, "trust me, one day, everything will make much more sense."

I let her go out of my arms. They turned around without saying a word and left.

I stood there in silence, in tears and observed them as they were leaving. I used my right fist, the same one I was planning to use as my main means of transportation for the next couple of years, and hit the wall with it as hard as I could.

I sat on the stairs, where no one could see me, and put my head between the palms. I cried like never before.

What kind of fucking son was I? How could I do that to them? To the people who gave me my life, who were always there for me? I was paying them back by going on a trip around the world, hitchhiking. Wasn't that the most selfish act a person could do?

"Bro, let's go," Filip told me and took me to his apartment before I managed to say goodbye to the remaining guests. During the whole ride I couldn't stop sobbing on the back seat.

He prepared his couch, on which I was supposed to spend my last night in Zagreb.

I checked my e-mails.

Hey big guy,

Your dream. It's finally coming true.

I'm sorry I haven't made it to Zagreb. Or a few months earlier to Bangladesh, even though I wanted to see you more than anything. Trust me, I wanted it. But I couldn't. Someday I'll tell you why.

But a piece of you is always with me.

Somewhere within me there's still a girl who was lying on the grass in that Berlin park, listening to a boy saying he loved her. And she's lying when she says she doesn't love him. And she did love him, and she still does, and she'll always love him. Despite the fact that they're always on the opposite side of the planet.

Think of me when you're watching the sunrise, when your toes are touching the Pacific, when an elephant steals your hat. Enjoy your dream. Because it is yours.

Maybe one day, we'll meet at my house, in a shabby hotel in India or somewhere in South America on a beach during the sunset. Whenever, it will happen. It has to.

Kiss,

Chloe

I wiped the tears off of my face with my palms and took a deep breath. I remembered the look she gave me when she was at my front door. The look I wanted to have for myself. The life I wanted to live. And which was now there, one night away.

I remembered quitting my job as a stockbroker, working in the juice bar, hosting CouchSurfers, first trips, a broken heart in Berlin, presentation about CS in Zagreb where I got the idea to create the Facebook page, wandering around Andalusia, organizing the hitchhiking race, appearing in the media, Bangladesh, meeting Tanja, finishing university, everything.

I knew that was it. That I was doing the right thing. That I had to follow my dream. That I didn't have any other choice. That I couldn't give up. That the instinct should give the final punch in the face of fear.

Hey little one,
Just to let you know – my dream is you.

Forever yours, T.

I put down the laptop and fell asleep.

Day 100(1).

I was awake even before the alarm went off, at 6:04.

ABOUT THE AUTHOR

Born in Zagreb, Croatia, on April 6th, 1985.

The rest you can read in the book.

SPECIAL THANKS TO:

- Everyone that has been a part of this story - family, friends, CS-ers, drivers, random people met on the street.

- The crew that worked with me on this book.

- Everyone that contributed to my crowdfunding campaign and made this book possible, especially:
  Miss Krassi Hristova
  Mrs Nancy Paiva
  Mr Tito Bhuiyan
  Mr Jefferey Dunn
  Mr David Marshall

- You, for reading this book.

Thank you, T.

Čiči - winner of the hitchhiking race.
foto: Marina Damjan

Fifteen of us, and Nina the dog.
foto: Marina Damjan

My dear Maria Juana.
foto: Marina Damjan

First sigths in Bangladesh.

Street admirers.

South Dhaka.

Workers in the textile factory.

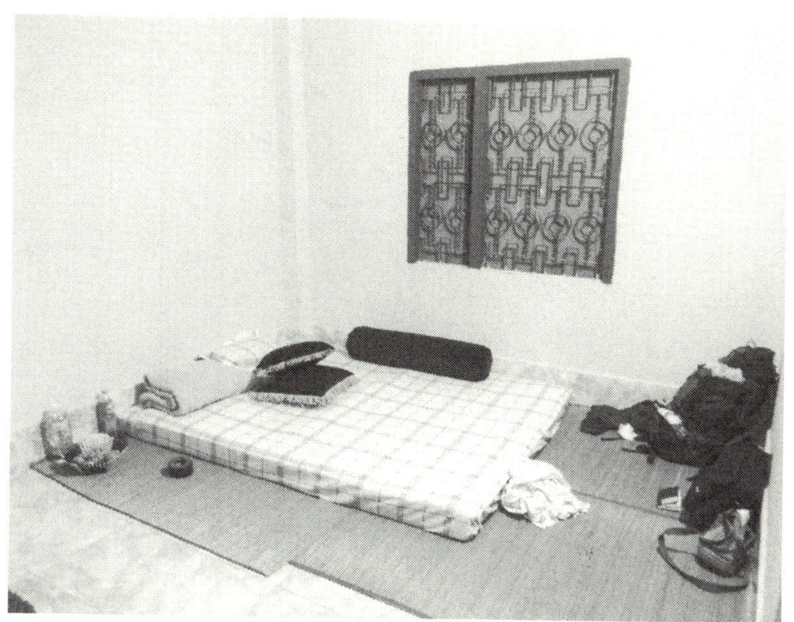

My room in Kusthia.

With Boss and couple of friends.

On the way to Shilaidaha.

Tagore's estate.

Woman and her baby.

My friends in Dhaka.

My drunk friends in Dhaka.

The wedding.

Samai and I.

Comilla.

With Sajid.

Eating like locals.

In the train.

April and Taya.

With local kids.

Another one.

Washing clothes in Kushtia.

Rickshaw driver.

In the kitchen.

With other gurus.

FREE HUGS hitchhiking.

On the way to Chloe.

64373960R00147